Lexcel Assessment Guide

Lexcel Assessment Guide

The Law Society

The Law Society

First edition published in 1997 as *The Assessment Guide*
Second edition published in 2001 as the *Lexcel Assessment Guide*

This third edition published in 2004 by the Law Society
113 Chancery Lane, London WC2A 1PL

ISBN 1–85328–921–3

Typeset by Columns Design Ltd., Reading
Printed by TJ International, Padstow, Cornwall

Contents

Preface

This publication sets out the information that will be required by practitioners, assessors and consultants on the 2004 version of the Lexcel standard. The aim has been to replace the former *Lexcel Assessment Guide*, which formed part of the previous edition of the *Lexcel Practice Excellence Kit*, and the *Guidelines for Assessors* which formed part of the Lexcel training materials. Both former publications are now consolidated into this work.

The *Lexcel Assessment Guide* should be read in conjunction with the *Lexcel Office Procedures Manual*, which has also been revised to take into account the 2004 version of the Lexcel standard.

The process of reviewing Lexcel was undertaken throughout 2003 by a revisions committee under the chairmanship of John Pickup, Council member and then chair of the Lexcel Assessment Panel. The other members of the panel were Alex Bannister (vice-chair of the Lexcel Assessment Panel), Simon Young (Council member), Brian Capstick (private practice representative), Sue Carter (Sole Practitioners Group), Stephen Rickitt (local government representative), Mark Spash (private practice representative) and James Sandbach (NACAB). In addition, two consultants were part of the committee – Matthew Moore (principal trainer in the Lexcel scheme) and Vicky Ling. Rupert Kendrick was consulted on computer use issues. The Law Society officers involved were Victor Olowe, Tracey Stanley and Iona Milton-Jones.

This publication has been the responsibility of the Lexcel Office who would wish to acknowledge the role of Matthew Moore and Vicky Ling in writing most of the contents.

February 2004

I The Lexcel scheme

Introduction to the scheme

The Practice Management Standards (PMS) are a set of requirements designed specifically with the needs of solicitors in mind.

The Lexcel scheme allows practices to undergo assessment by an independent assessor who can certify that the practice has complied with the core requirements of the PMS. The Lexcel certificate is awarded for three years, subject to satisfactory interim annual maintenance visits. The Law Society awards the certificate, and is the 'certificating body' for the scheme.

Assessments are carried out by specially trained assessors who are already qualified assessors of ISO9000 or Investors in People working with one of the established ISO9000 certification bodies or Regional Quality Centres. This has the added advantage of enabling practices, if they wish, to be assessed to one of these other standards at the same time as Lexcel, so saving time and resources.

By using experienced and qualified assessors from these bodies, we can ensure that assessments are conducted independently, fairly and uniformly and that the award of the Lexcel certificate is a mark of quality respected by clients. It should be noted that these organisations are themselves subject to rigorous quality control.

An organisation that has carried out advisory work for a practice will *not* be eligible to conduct any of its assessments. This applies to both employees and associates of the organisation in question.

Practices and all relevant personnel will be asked for consent for a search to be made of their indemnity insurance and disciplinary records prior to certification being awarded. If fraud or serious professional misconduct is revealed, the Law Society reserves the right to suspend, withdraw, withhold or defer certification, and/or to consider whether an assessment should be allowed to proceed.

The Law Society has a confidentiality agreement with the assessment bodies requiring staff members to keep all information confidential. Practices may also consider obtaining an independent agreement from their assessment body.

Details of the assessment bodies taking part in the scheme and information on how to apply for certification are available from the Lexcel Office, telephone: 020 7320 5749; address: The Law Society, 113 Chancery Lane, London WC2A 1PL or DX 56 London/Chancery Ln.

The Lexcel website address is **www.lexcel.lawsociety.org.uk**

Revisions to Lexcel

Since the launch of Lexcel in 1997, the Law Society has been closely monitoring the operation of the scheme and developments in the field of practice management. As a result, a number of amendments have been made to the scheme following extensive consultation with practices, assessors and various key individuals and interest groups within the profession and the Law Society.

The Lexcel standard has been rearranged into eight more balanced sections in place of the former six. There are new sections dealing with policies, client care, and supervision and risk management. The opportunity has also been taken to address issues that were not so pressing in 2000 at the time of the last revisions: computer use and combating money laundering are the most obvious examples. It is hoped that the changes will improve the benefits that practices receive from implementing the standard, as well as improving client confidence in the scheme.

An important change is the removal of the need for documented procedures in the case of a number of provisions. It is recognised that if compliance can be shown by other means, this may sometimes be appropriate.

A fuller comparison of the new contents of the standard appears as an appendix to this *Guide*.

The philosophy of assessment

The objective of Lexcel is to enhance the service given by a practice to its clients and to improve the management of the practice and the morale and motivation of its staff. In the case of firms in private practice this should enhance profitability.

Assessments are carried out to provide objective assurance that the core requirements of the PMS are being adhered to by the practice.

The assessor will seek to identify whether and how the practice is working to their core requirements. The guidance set out in the Assessment Criteria is intended to assist a practice in understanding and working towards the core requirements. The prescriptive aspects are contained in the requirements but the guidance itself is illustrative, and practices may demonstrate that they comply with the core requirements by other means.

Joint assessments to ISO9000 or Investors in People

For those practices wishing to apply for joint assessment of Lexcel with either ISO9000 or with Investors in People, a table has been produced showing how these standards overlap. Copies are included in the Lexcel information pack which is available from the Lexcel Office on 020 7320 5749.

Further information about ISO9000 is available from the relevant assessment centres or bodies. Copies of the ISO9000 Standard are available from:

> The British Standards Institution
> 389 Chiswick High Road
> London W4 4AL
>
> tel: 020 8996 9000
> fax: 020 8996 7400
> Standards Sales Information Line: 020 8996 9001

Further information about Investors in People is available from Regional Quality Centres or Learning and Skills Councils (LSCs), or from:

> Investors in People UK
> 7–10 Chandos Street
> London W1M 9DE
>
> tel: 020 7467 1900
> fax: 020 7636 2386

Details of those Investors in People and ISO9000 bodies which also offer Lexcel are available from the Lexcel Office on 020 7320 5749.

Lexcel and the Community Legal Service Quality Mark

The Legal Services Commission and the Lexcel Office will continue to consider the relationship between the new version of Lexcel and the Community Legal Service Quality Mark (CLSQM) in the light of operational changes to the CLSQM.

Lexcel assessment is directed at the wider needs of the profession. Practices that wish to consider CLSQM may be expected to comply with a number of additional requirements over and above those demanded by Lexcel. Compliance with the CLSQM is mandatory for those practices seeking to offer publicly funded work.

Who may apply for accreditation?

Lexcel is normally granted to a whole practice. All offices or branches of a practice will normally be expected to apply for certification at the same time.

Subject to satisfying the conditions set out below, local government, and commerce and industry practices may also apply for certification. The practice must:

- Have a defined structure and policies.
- Develop and maintain a marketing and business plan.
- Document responsibility for financial management procedures.
- Document the office facilities needed to provide a service to clients.
- Adopt arrangements for the recruitment, development and welfare of its personnel.
- Have supervision and operational risk management systems in place.
- Have a documented policy for client care.
- Have file and case management systems in place.

Where applicable, guidance on the application of Lexcel in local government practices, commerce and industry practices and sole practitioners is given in the guidance section of each requirement. Sole practitioners will also be able to obtain a Lexcel booklet entitled 'Lexcel: a Guide for Sole Practitioners', which contains useful information on how to implement the Standard.

Charges

A registration fee is payable directly to the Law Society and is based upon the number of partners (or fee-earners for local government, and commerce and industry practices) in the practice. The assessment body will charge the practice a fee based upon the duration of the assessment, which is influenced chiefly by the number of people in the practice and the number of branches.

Tables setting out assessment duration guidelines are included with the Lexcel information pack which is available from the Lexcel Office on 020 7320 5749.

Please bear in mind that the level of fees may vary between assessment bodies and it is advisable to obtain a number of quotes. Enquiries might also be made to see when an assessment will be possible and whether a single assessor or a team will be involved. The relevant bodies will be able to give an idea of their charges. If the intention is to apply for Investors in People at the same time as Lexcel, the practice may qualify for financial assistance. Further details are available from Regional Quality Centres or Learning and Skills Council.

II Applying for accreditation

The application process

This section sets out the steps that a practice will need to take in order to apply for Lexcel certification alone or jointly with another standard.

Preparing for the application

The practice seeking Lexcel certification will need to satisfy itself that it complies with the mandatory requirements of the PMS. Using the Self-Assessment Checklist (supplied with the Lexcel information pack) the practice can check the extent to which it meets these requirements. Any weaknesses identified should be put right.

During the self-assessment process, the practice will need to refer to the Assessment Criteria.

It may be necessary to repeat the self-assessment process a number of times before arriving at a satisfactory result.

The commitment scheme

The scheme has been developed to encourage firms to register their genuine commitment towards applying for Lexcel accreditation.

Previous experience has shown that firms are hesitant to apply for Lexcel until they are absolutely sure that the practice will fully comply with all the PMS. Quite often this is due to a lack of confidence, rather than an inability to meet the requirements of the standard. The aim of the commitment scheme is to enhance motivation and provide a definitive assessment deadline for a firm to work towards.

To register on the commitment scheme, a firm needs to complete a registration form, which can be obtained from the Lexcel Office. Once the form has been returned, a commitment scheme certificate will be issued to the firm. The Lexcel Office will then make periodic contact with the practice to provide support, establish that progress is still being made, and ensure that the intended assessment date will be met.

A further benefit available to the firms registered on the commitment scheme is the availability of a pre-application assessment.

Pre-application assessment

Historically, practices have employed Lexcel consultants and assessors to conduct diagnostic tests or 'dummy assessments' (at additional expense) to check Lexcel compliance. Any areas of compliance identified from this dummy or diagnostic assessment could not be credited to the practice once it had applied for Lexcel. This means practices incur additional expense in time and cost, since the assessment must be repeated following application. The pre-application assessment allows firms to undergo a dummy assessment, but to receive credit towards the final assessment for any of the PMS requirements that are met, thus reducing the burden of time and cost on the practice. To receive further information, please contact the Lexcel Office.

Choosing an assessment body

Details of Lexcel assessment bodies taking part in the scheme are included in the Lexcel information pack.

If the intention is to apply for Lexcel only, then it should make little difference which assessment body the practice chooses, as Lexcel will be assessed in a standard way. However, as mentioned previously, different assessment bodies have different fee structures.

The choice of assessment body will depend to a large extent on future plans for certification. If the practice currently has, or intends to apply for ISO9000 then it makes sense to choose an ISO9000 assessment body. If the preference is for Investors in People, then the practice should apply to its Regional Quality Centre or Learning Skills Council.

Applying for assessment

When the practice has satisfied itself that it meets the Lexcel requirements it should contact the Lexcel Office and request an information pack. The application pack includes status enquiry forms that gives the Lexcel Office the authority to check the practice's indemnity insurance and disciplinary records prior to the certificate being awarded.

The Law Society will consider the results of these checks before allowing a practice to proceed with the assessment. Practices should apply well in advance to ensure the checks are completed in time for their proposed assessment.

With the application form, the practice should enclose:

- some background information about the practice (a copy of the practice's brochure, should one exist, will normally be sufficient);
- a copy of the Self-Assessment Checklist, completed;
- for non-private practices, a letter authorising the application;
- signed status enquiry forms for the practice and all relevant personnel (relevant personnel are defined as all fee-earners, whether admitted as solicitors, or non-admitted, such as legal executives, barristers or trainee solicitors; non-fee-earning staff do *not* have to complete the status enquiry forms);
- details of any indemnity insurance or disciplinary history relevant to the application.

III The assessment process

The assessment

The Lexcel assessment is designed to ensure that:

- all the PMS core requirements are addressed within the practice;
- documentary evidence of this exists;
- procedures and processes are understood throughout the practice;
- the practice applies them and does so consistently.

The assessment process is entirely transparent.

The assessment criteria

The 'Assessment Criteria' section provides information concerning each mandatory requirement of the PMS. It contains:

- guidance on the manner in which a practice may meet the requirements;
- key issues to consider in each section;
- examples of typical documentation which may be used to show that the practice meets the requirement;
- examples of what would constitute a major or minor non-compliance in a particular area.

Planning the assessment

The assessor will arrange dates for the assessment with the practice's nominated Lexcel contact. During the assessment the assessor will visit each practice location and have meetings with the practice's representative, as required, to review progress.

The assessor will respect client and business confidentiality. Subject to this, the assessor will, on site:

- inspect documentary evidence and look at other relevant records;
- interview a representative cross-section of principals and staff to confirm that the necessary processes are in place and are understood;
- conduct case management audits with a selection of fee-earners.

Lexcel assessors undergo a quality-assured training programme to ensure that they apply the Lexcel standard according to national guidelines. However, they also need to be able

7

to exercise sufficient flexibility to use their professional judgement in the context of each assessment. Consistency of assessment is monitored by the Law Society and anomalies are investigated.

It is important that an appropriate distinction is maintained between assessment and consultancy. If a practice uses a consultant to advise on implementation of the standard, that individual must not carry out the Lexcel assessment for the practice.

Assessors must confine themselves to the requirements of Lexcel when conducting an assessment and must not assess procedures which fall outside it.

Assessors are required to respect the duty of confidentiality which solicitors owe to their clients. The section on 'Client confidentiality and the contents of files' (page 13) gives detailed information on the practical issues that may affect assessments.

Practices may not be able to allow inspection of some or all files. If a client has refused to allow disclosure to an assessor, the practice may not be able to show the assessor a letter of refusal as the letter would contain the client's name. Assessors will need to have an understanding of the way in which they can identify files where clients' consent has been obtained, at an early stage.

When seeking certification, the onus is on the practice to satisfy the assessor that it meets the standard. If the practice cannot allow access to case files, it will have to work with the assessor to identify other ways in which satisfactory evidence can be established. It is likely that alternative methods will take longer to assess, and may increase the cost of any assessment. The assessor should advise the practice accordingly.

What happens during the assessment

Assessments typically include the following processes:

a: The assessor becomes familiar with the systems by which the applicant practice is implementing the Lexcel standard.
b: The assessor seeks objective evidence that the required systems and procedures are in effective operation.

The most significant part of the time spent during the assessment will be on the premises of the practice applying for certification. Assessors differ in that some familiarise themselves with the systems on the premises while others carry out some familiarisation off-site. It is common practice, however, to conduct an initial 'desk-top' audit of the office manual before the visit. Assessors may also spend time following the assessment in completing their report and reporting back to the Law Society. Assessors should ensure that practices are aware that any costs involved in so doing are included in the cost quotation for the assessment.

The processes involved in the assessment will be as described above regardless of where they take place.

Obtaining a cost quotation for the assessment

The assessor will need sufficient information from the practice before a quotation can be prepared. Relevant information would include: the number of categories of law offered by the practice; the number and location of sites; numbers of fee-earners, partners, solicitors; numbers of support staff; whether the practice holds any other quality certification; whether the assessment is Lexcel alone or will be combined with Investors in People or ISO9000.

Since the length and cost of an assessment will be significantly affected if the assessor cannot see case files, assessors will need to establish whether this is likely to be a significant factor at an early stage.

The cost quotation *should not* include the annual registration fee paid by the practice to the Law Society. Details of the registration fee can be obtained from the Lexcel information brochure.

Duration of assessment

The main factor affecting the length of assessment is the number of fee-earners. Other significant factors include: numbers of support staff; number and type of sites; degree of differentiation in work patterns between departments; degree of documentation available to support the systems; whether the auditor has access to case files; familiarity of the practice being audited with quality systems, e.g. ISO9000, Investors in People, or the Community Legal Service Quality Mark.

The time estimates given below are guidelines only and are not prescriptive. The actual time taken for assessments is monitored by the Law Society and the guidelines are reviewed in the light of experience. In the course of monitoring, any anomalies will be investigated.

The guidelines below include all the work leading up to the assessor's recommendation at the end of the assessment on the applicant's premises. They include preparation and final reporting to the Law Society.

Geographical location of offices and degree of centralisation of systems will affect the duration of assessments in multi-office practices.

The likely duration of assessment can be ascertained by adding the total obtained from Table 1 (overleaf) to the total obtained from Table 2. It is very unlikely that the length of assessments can be reduced at the bottom end of the scale. The Lexcel Assessment Panel has rebuked assessors for such conduct in the past, which may in extreme cases require a re-visit.

Assessors are reminded that the duration of assessments may be reduced where a practice has been assessed against a quality standard such as Investors in People, ISO9000, CharterMark or the Specialist Quality Mark (SQM) within six months of having their Lexcel assessment. An overlap table can be obtained from the Lexcel office, which details the overlaps between Lexcel and other quality standards.

Table 1: Duration indicator – by number of fee-earners

Fee-earners in office	Person days: main office	Additional person days: branch offices
1–5	1	0.5
6–10	1.5	0.5
11–20	2	1
21–30	2.5	1
31–40	3	1.5
41–50	3.5	2
50+	4	3

Table 2: Duration indicator – by number of support staff

Support staff in office	Person days: main office	Additional person days: branch offices
1–30	0.5	0.5
31+	0.75	0.75

Example: estimating duration of assessment

Main Office has 59 fee-earners and 40 support staff, Branch Office A has 15 fee-earners and 5 support staff and Branch Office B has 4 fee-earners and 2 support staff.

Duration at Main Office:	fee-earners – 4 days; support staff – 0.75 day
Duration at Branch Office A:	fee-earners – 1 day; support staff – 0.5 day
Duration at Branch Office B:	fee-earners – 0.5 day; support staff: 0.5 day
Total duration:	*7.25 days*

Interview sample sizes

Assessors will interview individuals during the course of the assessment. Those interviewed may have a designated role, such as supervisor, senior partner, trainee, newly recruited staff member, etc., or they may be selected on a random basis to verify that a procedure is in effective operation.

Samples will depend on the number of legal categories offered by a practice, the numbers of people working within each department and the degree of compliance observed in the initial sample. If an assessor notes apparent non-compliance, the sample may need to be larger than the initial sample to demonstrate a high degree of compliance. The Law Society may also direct that sample sizes may need to be increased at assessment, up to the recommended maximum guidelines for the size of that practice, where the results of the status enquiry checks indicate this is necessary.

The interview sample sizes given in Table 3 are guidelines. Assessors will make decisions based on the circumstances of the practice being assessed, such as those set out above.

Actual sample sizes will be monitored by the Law Society and the guidelines will be revised in the light of experience. In the course of monitoring, any anomalies will be investigated.

Table 3: Interview sample size guidelines

Total number of partners, principals, fee-earners and support staff in the practice	Sample (%)	
	Fee-earners	**Support**
1–5	70	40
6–15	50	30
16–25	35	15
26–50	25	10
51–75	15	7
76–100	12	5
101–125	8	3
126–500	6	2.5
501–1000	3	1
1001+	2	0.5

Case file samples

An assessor should audit at least five open files for each fee-earner in the sample. If the fee-earner undertakes more than one category of work, the assessor should look at files from all categories if possible.

Fewer files may be audited if the individual has a small number of files. This is typically because the fee-earner is senior and conducts a small number of complex cases, or because the fee-earner is junior and is developing a caseload under supervision.

The number of files audited may need to be increased if any fee-earner has conduct of a large number or percentage of the practice's total open file stock, or if initial assessment appears to indicate a high level of non-compliance.

Files selected should cover all the areas of law in which the practice offers services. A practice with SQM, for example, would not normally need to have those areas of overlap with the SQM examined.

The time taken to audit files will vary according to whether the assessor has direct access to them. The assessment will be quicker if the assessor can identify key issues for him/herself rather than having to ascertain the information from the fee-earner during an interview.

An increasing number of practices use computerised case management systems, so that a case record may be held partly on computer and partly on paper. Where this is so, and the assessor has access to case files, he or she will wish to see the computer records as well as the paper file.

Inspection of documentation

During the self-assessment process, the practice must have identified internal documentation showing how it meets the Lexcel requirements. It should make this documentation available to the assessor on request. A major part may be in the practice's office manual. Note that to have an office manual is a mandatory Lexcel requirement, though it can be in electronic format.

Documents submitted as evidence that the practice complies with a requirement should be self-evident, current and in use generally within the practice.

The assessor will study the documentary evidence submitted. Practices need not produce information that is commercially sensitive or client confidential. Indeed, to protect practice or client confidentiality, a practice may submit documents in such a form that anonymity is assured.

Assessment interviews

There are three main reasons for conducting interviews:

- to clarify points that may arise during the review of written evidence;
- to obtain more evidence (where the documentation only forms part of the evidence required to demonstrate compliance, or where documentation is not appropriate);
- to check that relevant personnel understand processes and procedures and apply them consistently.

The assessor may request a listing for each location, of principals and staff with details of names, job titles, departments and, if possible, length of service. The assessor will choose a representative cross-section of personnel for interview from the list supplied with the application. The assessor will notify the practice of the names of those selected for interview before any site visit. The numbers and roles of the personnel selected for interview will depend upon the size of the practice, its type and its structure.

Conscious of a practice's operational requirements, the assessor will fix the times of interviews for the convenience of those concerned. The assessor will agree to replacements for personnel who are, for operational reasons, unavailable for interview or reschedule the interview.

Interviews will be informal and confidential. Assessors will request that practices provide a quiet and secure room so that the interviews may take place in private.

Case management audits

The assessor will identify a selection of case files. The assessor will question the relevant fee-earner about these files, to check that all requirements of the case management standard are being met. This review will give the fee-earner an opportunity to explain how the procedures are working.

Client confidentiality and the contents of files

A number of the requirements set out in the Assessment Criteria concern the relationship between a practice and its clients and the way in which the practice maintains a record of that relationship. The lists of 'Typical Documentation' for those requirements include client care letters, attendance notes, client correspondence and case files. These are all documents confidential to the client, which the practice cannot disclose to an assessor without prior consent of the client. Solicitors owe a duty of confidentiality to clients in law and in conduct.

Practices are encouraged to obtain consent from their clients to disclosure of the contents of these documents to assessors. However, if a practice considers that it is not practical to ask for that consent, the assessment of the relevant requirement will be carried out on the basis that evidence will be gathered by the assessor through asking a fee-earner to find relevant documents in the case file, and evidence of compliance will be given by the fee-earner confirming that a document of the sort needed to show compliance is in fact present on the file. Care should be taken to avoid disclosing confidential information concerning the client's identity and affairs.

The following notes A to E apply if a practice proposes to allow assessors to inspect case files.

A. *Need for consent*

The best evidence that the client's consent has been given is a note on the file to that effect signed by the client. It may, however, be sufficient for consent to be obtained by 'exception reporting', i.e. clients are invited to notify the practice only if they wish to withhold their consent. Practitioners should be aware that this latter method of seeking consent has not been tested in the courts and so no guarantee can be given that it would be adequate; the ultimate decision must be one for the practice, depending on all the circumstances.

Subject to the above, the Law Society recommends:

a: the client must be notified of the possibility of inspection by quality assessors and the reasons for such inspection; and
b: either:

    i: the client must expressly consent to the inspection and must be informed that he or she can withdraw consent at any time; or
    ii: the client must be informed that he or she should notify the practice at any time if the client wishes to withhold consent; and

c: the solicitor (who is under a continuing duty to act in the best interests of the client) must at all times consider whether the client should have his or her file protected from inspection, whether or not the client has previously consented to its disclosure.

B. *Obtaining consent*

Solicitors practices which seek certification to Lexcel, or to other externally assessed standards, will normally have a written procedure for taking instructions. These will provide that every client receives a letter, or other document, confirming the practice's terms of business, basis of charging and named contact in the event of any problem with the service provided. This would normally be an ideal opportunity to provide the information and to seek the consent referred to above.

The precise manner in which consent is requested will vary according to the individual circumstances of the client and the nature of the retainer. For example, it would be inappropriate to seek consent to disclosure at the outset of the retainer:

a: if particular sensitivity is required in handling the matter, e.g. when preparing a deathbed will, in a domestic violence emergency or when seeing a person very recently bereaved;

b: in cases of urgency when it is not practical to give the client a proper opportunity to consider the question of confidentiality.

In other cases, it might be possible to obtain the client's consent in respect of a series of future transactions to be carried out on the client's behalf or as part of standing terms of business with a regular client.

C. *Initial assessment*

When an initial assessment takes place there may be clients whose files were opened before the practice started notifying clients of the possibility of inspection. If the proportion of these files means that they need to be included in the initial inspection, a letter must be written to all clients informing them of the possibility of the inspection, and either:

a: seeking the client's express consent to the inspection, and informing the client that he or she may withdraw consent at any time; or

b: advising the client of his or her rights to notify the practice at any time if the client wishes to withhold consent to inspection.

D. *No consent*

If:

a: the client refuses consent; or

b: it is appropriate to treat the file as one for which consent has been refused

the practice must tell the assessor that the file is not available for inspection.

E. Withholding certain files

Circumstances in which it may be appropriate to treat the file as one for which consent has been refused include:

a: if the case involves allegations about behaviour which might seriously prejudice the client's reputation or which might offend public decency, e.g. serious criminal charges and some matrimonial and child care proceedings;
b: if the client lacks the capacity to appreciate properly the consequences of giving consent (e.g. a minor, a client with difficulty understanding written English or suffering mental incapacity);
c: if the case involves matters of current or future financial, commercial or market sensitivity (price-sensitive information).

Non-compliances

A non-compliance is recorded where an assessor cannot find evidence that a requirement of the standard is being met. There are two types of non-compliance which may be recorded:

*   **minor:** where the non-compliance can be corrected within 21 days *and* the assessor is able to accept documentary evidence sent by the practice that corrective action has been carried out;
*   **major:** where the non-compliance will take longer than 21 days to correct *or* the assessor has to visit the practice again in order to establish that corrective action has been carried out.

In some circumstances assessors may note areas for improvement. For example: where a non-compliance cannot be fully rectified as an activity has not been carried out at the correct time; where non-compliances have been identified within the practice due to an individual who has left the practice, although subsequent corrective action has been taken; where there is evidence that a system may be breaking down although no non-compliance is identified; or as suggestions for improving, or recording best practice.

Assessors are also actively encouraged to note areas of good practice and congratulate the organisation where appropriate.

Accreditation

After the assessment has been completed there will be a meeting with the relevant members of the practice at which the assessor will provide feedback on the assessment.

The assessor will inform the practice of his or her recommendation at the end of the assessment visit.

Four recommendations are possible:

a: The assessor requires documentary evidence of corrective action within 21 days of the assessment before a recommendation for certification can be made.

b: A re-visit to check corrective action is required within three months of the assessment before a recommendation for certification can be made.

c: Certification premature – further full assessment is required (with an indication of the likely timescale).

d: Certification/continue certification.

It is accepted that the assessment is carried out on a sampling basis and an assessor is unlikely to observe all non-compliances within the practice. The recommendation for certification is based on the findings relating to the sample.

The assessor will produce a written report and recommend whether to grant a certificate. The report will include a summary of the evidence collected and state whether the practice meets all the PMS core requirements. The report will be sent to the Law Society's Lexcel Office, which will decide whether to grant Lexcel certification. In some circumstances the report will need to be referred to the Lexcel Assessment Panel who will decide whether to grant Lexcel certification.

Annual maintenance visits

Following the initial assessment the Law Society issues a certificate to confirm that the practice meets the Lexcel requirements. The certificate is valid for three years subject to annual maintenance visits to ensure that the Standards are still being met. A full reassessment is carried out after three years.

Annual maintenance visits (AMVs) should be held before or during the month of the anniversary of the issue of the certificate. The **whole** process must have been completed each year by the end of the month of the anniversary of the issue of the certificate. Practices are therefore advised to have their AMV and reassessments carried out prior to, or early in the month of, the anniversary of assessment to give time for corrective action, if necessary.

If a simultaneous monitoring visit falls due for Investors in People or ISO9000 before the Lexcel AMV, the Lexcel assessment can be brought forward to bring the two into alignment. However, practices will need to keep the earlier date for their subsequent AMV and reassessment or there would be a gap of more than one year between assessments.

Practices will have a maximum of one month's leeway on either side of the due date for the annual maintenance assessment or reassessment to take place, subject to the above paragraphs.

During an AMV, compliance against all the Lexcel requirements will be reviewed. However, the number of case files reviewed and interviews conducted will be approximately half of the number in the guidelines for an initial assessment.

Factors affecting the duration of the annual maintenance assessment will include the number and type of non-compliances previously identified and the degree of change to the practice structure or staff since the last visit.

The procedures for status enquiry checks is different for AMVs. Checks will only be carried out for any new starters since the date of the practice's initial assessment (or previous AMV). However, status enquiry checks would be carried out for all fee-earners at the full re-assessment.

However, the Law Society will be entitled to carry out further status enquiry checks about the practice at its discretion at any time during the duration of the Lexcel certificate. This is to maintain the overall integrity of the system, and retain a safeguard for further checks at the Assessment Panel's discretion.

The Law Society will therefore only require status enquiry forms from:

a: any new partners and admitted fee-earners;
b: any new non-admitted fee-earners; or
c: fee-earners if they have changed status, e.g. non-admitted fee-earners have become admitted or admitted fee-earners have become partners.

Practices will be asked to enclose a staff list, when returning the AMV form, indicating new starters since the original assessment or last AMV, together with their status enquiry forms.

Practices are reminded that they are under a continuing duty to inform the Lexcel Office immediately of any circumstances involving the practice, or any individual working at the practice involved in fraud, serious professional misconduct or a flagrant breach of the PMS.

Mergers and de-mergers

Where the practice has recently merged with another practice, or opened a new branch or branches, those parts of the practice which have not previously been assessed will be subject to a full assessment. Such assessment will take place either concurrently with the AMV, or at a time to be agreed between the Law Society and the practice. A Lexcel certificate will be awarded for each new branch once all the branches of the practice have been successfully assessed. The additional certificates will be valid for the same duration as the original certificate to enable the future AMVs or full assessments to coincide for the whole practice.

Where a branch has de-merged from the original practice, a fresh application will be required from the new practice. The new practice must surrender any certificate and logos from the date of de-merger. A fresh assessment will be required for the new practice, although credit will be given in relation to the previous award including status enquiry checks and the results of the previous assessment. The extent of this credit depends on the individual circumstances of the practice, and the time elapsed from first assessment or AMV.

Fraud/dishonesty discovered during an assessment

If an assessor suspects as a result of findings during an assessment that there may be fraud, dishonest activity or serious breaches of the Solicitors' Professional Conduct Rules within the practice, the assessor must without delay contact the Lexcel Office for advice as to how to proceed.

Withdrawal or suspension of certification

The Law Society's Lexcel Assessment Panel may decide to defer, withdraw, withhold or suspend certification in respect of the whole of any practice if the practice is found, or suspected to be, in flagrant breach of Lexcel, or to have committed a fraud or serious professional misconduct.

Practices and assessors are reminded that an assessment should *not* be carried out without clearance to proceed first having been granted by the Law Society. Without this clearance the practice runs the risk of having to pay for the cost of assessment and not being awarded Lexcel by the Lexcel Assessment Panel.

The Panel may require a full reassessment as a condition of reviewing a suspended or withdrawn certificate.

Appeals and complaints

If a practice wishes to appeal against a recommendation not to award or renew a certificate, it has the right of appeal to the Lexcel Appeals Panel. Details of the Lexcel appeal process can be obtained from the Lexcel Office.

Similarly, the Lexcel Office will consider complaints about the way in which the assessment has been conducted, or the assessment bodies involved.

IV The Lexcel standard 2004

Introduction

Organisations wishing to be recognised as meeting the Lexcel standard will need to show compliance with the eight sections of the standard. The application of the requirements will vary from practice to practice and will need to take into account all the special circumstances of each organisation. The aim of the standard is to enable practices to address the improvements that are appropriate and gain public recognition for having done so.

The objective of Lexcel is to enhance the service given by a practice to its clients and to improve the management of the practice and the morale and motivation of its staff.

Lexcel encourages practices to consult with clients to ensure that the views of the users of legal services have an impact on the way the service is delivered. There is an emphasis within the standard on continuous improvement.

There is reference in the standard to 'policies', 'processes', 'procedures' and 'plans'.

- A 'policy' is a general approach taken within the practice to the issue in question. A policy defines why a particular approach is adopted by the practice. Since it is only a general approach there may be stated exceptions from it, but it would be assumed that the policy will apply unless otherwise stated. An example from the standard is that practices are required to have a written policy in relation to client care (see section 7.1).
- A 'process' is a description of the sequence of related activities required to achieve desired outputs. A process must be observable even if there is no documented procedure requiring it to occur. An example is the requirement for an induction process at section 5.4. There is no requirement for a documented procedure in relation to induction, but it must be observable nonetheless.
- A 'procedure' is a written description of how an activity will occur within the practice. A procedure describes the steps that staff should follow in order to complete an activity. At an assessment, a procedure can only be said to be complied with if the assessor can observe that the procedure contained in the practice's documentation is in effective operation.
- A 'plan' is an outline of where a practice desires to be in the future and describes how it intends to arrive at that destination. A plan can be described as a map which supports practices to arrive at their desired destination in the future. An example is the requirement for marketing and business plans which could be combined in one document, at section 2.1. In general the Lexcel standard permits practices to develop plans in the manner and detail that the firm considers appropriate, assuming a basic level of adequacy.

Most organisations will document all procedures within an office manual, but there is no reason why they should not be set out in a number of different sources.

For ease of reference the term 'practice' is used throughout the standard. This should be taken to include any organisation that can be subject to the standard, including partnerships, limited liability partnerships, sole practices, incorporated law firms and legal departments. Various provisions of the standard may be inapplicable to certain types of practice, in which case they should be excluded, e.g. time recording may not be applicable in a local authority practice. The Lexcel Office provides guidance on the application of the standard to particular forms of practice.

The standard consists mostly of mandatory requirements, which are indicated by the use of the words 'will' or 'must'. There are also some optional requirements, which will be appropriate in most cases but are not mandatory; these are indicated by the use of the word 'should'.

The standard

1   STRUCTURES AND POLICIES

1.1   Practices will have documentation setting out the legal framework under which they operate.

1.2   Consideration should be given to the most appropriate business structure and this should be kept under review as part of the business planning process (section 2).

1.3   Practices will have a risk management strategy or framework.

1.4   Practices will have a written quality policy. This is a high level document setting out the organisation's commitment to quality and overall policy. Practices will also have documented procedures as set out in this standard, which will be distributed and published throughout the practice showing:

a: The role that the quality system plays in the overall strategy of the practice.
b: Who has responsibility for the management of the quality system.

1.5   There must be one designated individual who has particular responsibility for the quality system. Practices must be able to show that this individual has sufficient authority and seniority to raise concerns regarding the quality system and to have any such issues resolved.

1.6   There must be a review of the operation of the quality system at least annually and a process for people within the practice to suggest improvements to the system. The review must show the part that the quality system is intended to play in the future strategy of the practice over the next 12 months at least.

1.7   Practices will document procedures on non-discrimination, and have regard to guidance from the Law Society on non-discrimination in accepting instructions from clients, the use of experts and counsel and the provision of services to clients.

1.8   Practices will document procedures on equality and diversity including recruitment and employment procedures and have regard to guidance on equality and diversity issued by the Law Society from time to time.

1.9   Practices will have documented procedures to ensure compliance with money laundering legislation. The documented procedures should cover:

a: The appointment of a 'Nominated Officer' usually referred to as a Money Laundering Reporting Officer (MLRO).
b: Reporting of suspicious circumstances within the practice and by the MLRO to the authorities.

c: Identification checking.

d: Partner and staff training in anti-money laundering awareness.

e: The proper maintenance of records.

Any exemptions to these requirements must be stated in the practice's documented procedures.

1.10   Practices providing services to clients in relation to property transactions will have documented procedures in relation to the avoidance of involvement in mortgage fraud.

1.11   Practices will have a documented procedure in relation to data protection compliance issues.

1.12   Practices will have a documented policy in relation to the health and safety of partners, staff and visitors to the practice.

2   STRATEGY, THE PROVISION OF SERVICES AND MARKETING

2.1   Practices will develop and maintain a marketing and a business plan.

2.2   Practices will document the services they wish to offer, the client groups to be served, how services are to be provided (including any special features) and the way in which services are designed to meet client needs.

2.3   The documents, required by section 2.1 must be reviewed every six months and the review must be documented. The services and marketing plan or documentation required by section 2.2 must be produced or reviewed at least annually and must be current at the time of any assessment.

3.   FINANCIAL MANAGEMENT

3.1   Practices will document responsibility for financial management procedures.

3.2   Practices will be able to provide documentary evidence of their financial management processes, including:

a: Annual budget (including, where appropriate, any capital expenditure proposed).

b: Variance analysis conducted at least quarterly of income and expenditure against budgets.

c: Annual profit and loss or income and expenditure accounts (certificated or audited accounts).

d: Annual balance sheet.

e: Annual cash or funds flow forecast.

f: Quarterly variance analysis at least of cashflow.

Financial management data is best evidenced by showing all appropriate data or paperwork to assessors, but practices may decline to do so if they wish. In such cases the assessor will consider other evidence that is available, including correspondence from the practice's auditors and interviews with the partners and/or managers.

3.3   Practices will have a time recording process which enables the accurate measurement of time spent on matters for billing purposes and/or management analysis of the cost effectiveness of work and the efficiency of the practice.

4   FACILITIES AND IT

4.1   Practices will document the office facilities needed to provide a service to clients, including:

a: The use of premises and equipment, including security and related health and safety issues.
b: Photocopying, including maintenance and support.
c: Arrangements for clients to visit the offices, including reception, directions and car parking, if appropriate.
d: Staff facilities.
e: Mail, fax and other communication arrangements.
f: Procedures for the handling of financial transactions.

4.2   Practices will conduct a documented review of health and safety issues at least annually. They must show that it has received due consideration by top management and implementation has been acted upon or is planned, as appropriate.

4.3   There should be a business continuity plan envisaging the nature of catastrophic events that could beset the practice and the contingency plans that should be put into effect should they become necessary.

4.4   Practices will have a plan for IT use setting out the use of IT facilities within the practice and any planned changes. The IT plan should cover:

a: Responsibility for IT purchasing, installation, maintenance, support and training.
b: The current and planned applications within the practice of IT.
c: A data protection compliance statement in relation to staff, clients and others and registration with the Information Commissioner.
d: Compliance with all appropriate regulations and requirements.
e: User safety, see also 4.2 above.
f: Appropriate use of e-mail and attachments, both externally and internally, including storage of messages and the implications of not observing such procedures.
g: Computer data and system back up, to the extent not covered in any disaster recovery plan.

The IT plan must address at least a period of the current or next 12 months and may form part of the practice's overall strategy documentation, the office manual, or a separate document.

4.5   Practices will document arrangements for legal research and library facilities, whether in the practice or externally and whether through books and periodicals or computer-based services. A process must exist for the updating and sharing of legal and professional information.

4.6   Practices will maintain an office manual collating information on office practice, which must be available to all members of the practice. Practices will document their arrangements to:

a: Note each page with the date and/or issue.
b: Review the manual at least annually.
c: Update the manual and record the date of amendments.

5   PEOPLE MANAGEMENT

5.1   Practices will have a plan for the recruitment, development and welfare of their personnel, including:

a: Likely recruitment needs, whether for the practice as a whole, its departments or offices, which may form part of the practice's overall business plan or departmental or other operational plans.

b: Training and development.

c: Welfare and entitlements.

5.2 Practices will list the tasks to be undertaken by all personnel within the practice – including partners – and document the skills, knowledge and experience required for individuals to fulfil their role satisfactorily, usually in the form of a person specification and job description.

5.3 Practices will have procedures to deal effectively with recruitment into the practice, including:

a: The identification of vacancies.

b: The drafting of consequential job documentation, usually in the form of a job description.

c: Methods of attracting candidates and applicants.

d: Selection methods used.

e: Storage of interview notes.

f: Provision of information by way of feedback to unsuccessful candidates.

g: Any use of medical examination and/or references.

h: Confirmation of job offers.

i: Maintenance of communication during the pre-joining period and starting instructions.

5.4 Practices will conduct an appropriate induction process to cover:

a: The practice's aims.

b: Management structure and the individual's job responsibilities.

c: Terms and conditions of employment, personal and banking details for personnel records.

d: Initial and future training requirements.

e: Key policies, including equality and diversity and client care and office procedures.

5.5 The induction process must occur within a reasonable period of time of taking up the role.

5.6 Appropriate induction processes must apply when existing personnel transfer roles within the practice.

5.7 Practices will operate a process for:

a: An annual review at least of responsibilities, objectives and performance for all partners and staff members.

b: Written appraisal records, which will be confidential to the jobholder and named persons under the practice's data protection policy and may be inspected as evidence of compliance only with the consent of the jobholder.

c: An annual review at least of the training and development needs of all personnel within the practice, recorded in an individual training and development plan.

5.8 Practices will ensure that appropriate training is provided to personnel within the practice in accordance with its policy on training and development. Training may be arranged on an in-house or external basis and may be on-line or through more traditional means. Where appropriate the training should be recognised for CPD purposes under the scheme operated by the Law Society of England and Wales or other professional body or bodies.

6   SUPERVISION AND OPERATIONAL RISK MANAGEMENT

6.1   Practices will have a written description of their management structure which designates the responsibilities of individuals and their accountability. This will be updated within three months of any change.

6.2   There will be a named supervisor for each area of work undertaken by the practice. A supervisor may be responsible for more than one area of work. The supervisor must have appropriate experience of the work supervised and be competent to guide and assist others.

6.3   Practices will have processes to ensure that supervision of all staff, both legal and support staff, is effective. Issues which should receive consideration may include:

a: Checks on incoming and outgoing post, including e-mails and faxes.
b: Departmental, team and office meetings and communication structures.
c: Reviews of matter print-outs in order to ensure good financial controls and the appropriate allocation of workloads.
d: The exercise of devolved powers in publicly funded work.

6.4   Practices will have processes to ensure the effective supervision of legal work, to include:

a: The availability of adequate supervision.
b: Appropriate procedures to allocate new work and reallocate existing work if necessary.

6.5   Practices will have procedures to ensure that all those doing legal work check their files regularly for inactivity to avoid client dissatisfaction and possible claims arising from delay.

6.6   Practices will have procedures for regular, independent file reviews, of either the management of the file or its substantive legal content, or both. The number and frequency of such reviews will be documented. There is no requirement that designated supervisors should conduct all such reviews in person, but they will need to show that they control or monitor the process and that the process is effective.

In relation to file reviews, practices will have procedures to ensure that:

a: A record of the file review is kept on the matter file and centrally, whether for the practice or office as a whole or by team or department.
b: Any corrective action which is identified in a file review must be actioned within 28 days and verified by the reviewer.
c: There is a review at least annually of the data generated by file reviews, which will contribute to the review of risk assessment data (section 6.7f).

6.7   For the purposes of this section, operational risk management is the control and reduction of prosecutions, claims and client complaints against the practice. Practices will ensure that procedures are in place to:

a: Designate one overall risk manager for the practice with sufficient seniority, to be able to identify and deal with all risk issues which may arise.
b: Establish appropriate reporting arrangements to ensure that risk issues are appreciated and addressed.
c: Maintain lists of work that the practice will and will not undertake including any steps to be taken when work is declined on grounds that it falls outside acceptable risk levels. This information should be communicated to all staff and should be updated regularly.
d: Maintain details of the generic risks and causes of claims associated with the area(s) of work that is/are undertaken by the practice. This information must be adequately communicated to all staff.

e: Manage instructions which may be undertaken even though they have a higher risk profile than the norm for the practice including unusual supervisory and reporting requirements or contingency planning.

f: Conduct at least an annual review of all risk assessment data generated within the practice, including claims records, an analysis of client complaints trends and data generated by file reviews. The practice should identify remedial action, which should then be reviewed at management level in the practice.

6.8   Operational risk needs to be considered in all matters before, during and after the processing of instructions. Before the matter is undertaken the adviser must:

a: Consider if a new client and/or matter should be accepted by the practice, in accordance with section 8.2 below.

b: Assess the risk profile of all new instructions and notify the risk manager in accordance with procedures under 6.7 of any unusual or high risk considerations in order that appropriate action may be taken.

During the retainer the fee-earner must:

c: Consider any change to the risk profile of the matter from the client's point of view and report and advise on such circumstances without delay, informing the risk manager if appropriate.

d: Inform the client in all cases where an adverse costs order is made against the practice in relation to the matter in question.

At the end of the matter the fee-earner must:

e: Undertake a concluding risk assessment by considering if the client's objectives have been achieved and if the client could fairly complain or make a claim for damages in relation to the service provided.

f: Notify the risk manager of all such circumstances in accordance with documented procedures without delay.

7   CLIENT CARE

7.1   Practices will have a documented policy for client care, which will include:

a: The practice's commitment to provide services to clients in an appropriate manner.

b: Procedures to ensure compliance with Practice Rule 15 and its accompanying code in relation to client care and costs information.

7.2   Practices will have processes to ensure that clients are informed in writing of the terms of business under which instructions are received and will be handled, including:

a: The name and status of the fee-earner and the person(s) responsible for overall supervision.

b: Whom the client should approach in the event of a problem with the service provided.

c: The basis under which charges will be calculated including the best information possible on the likely overall costs of the matter.

The information required by this section should usually be provided in writing unless there are professional considerations that make this unsuitable in any particular matter.

There must be a record of any standing terms of business with regular clients, such as many commercial clients. The practice must be able to produce such terms in relation to the issues covered by this section.

7.3   Practices will operate a written complaints handling procedure that:

a: Is made readily available and accessible to clients when it is apparent that they may wish to have recourse to it.

b: Defines what the practice regards as a complaint and sets out how to identify and respond to complaints.

c: Records and reports centrally all complaints received from clients.

d: Identifies the cause of any problem of which the client has complained, offering any appropriate redress, and correcting any unsatisfactory procedures.

Practices must conduct reviews at least annually of complaints data and trends, such review(s) forming part of the review of risk assessment under 6.7f above.

7.4   Practices must conduct an annual review to check that the practice's commitment to provide quality services is being met in the perception of clients.

8   FILE AND CASE MANAGEMENT

8.1   Practices will document how client enquiries in relation to possible instructions are handled, with particular regard to:

a: The treatment of telephone enquiries.

b: Clients who enquire in person in the reception area, including confidentiality.

c: Enquiries by correspondence and e-mail.

8.2   Practices will document how decisions will be made whether to accept new instructions from existing clients or instructions from clients who have not instructed the practice before.

8.3   Practices will document their arrangements to ensure that conflicts of interest are identified and acted upon in an appropriate manner. Although this is a particular consideration when receiving instructions it may also be an issue later in the matter, as when third parties are subsequently joined in proceedings.

8.4   At the outset of the matter the fee-earner will establish:

a: As full an understanding as possible of the client's requirements and objectives (where incomplete this must be supplemented subsequently).

b: A clear explanation of the issues raised and the advice given.

c: What the fee-earner will do and in what timescale.

d: Whether the fee-earner is the appropriate person to deal with the matter or whether it should be referred to a colleague.

e: Method of funding, including the availability or suitability of insurance, trade union benefits, conditional or contingency fee arrangements, or costs insurance products.

f: Whether the intended action would be merited on a cost benefit analysis and whether, in public funding cases, the guidance in the funding code would be satisfied.

The issues covered in a–f above must be confirmed to the client, ordinarily in writing, unless it would be appropriate not to do so under the Solicitors' Costs Information and Client Care Code. In all cases a note of these issues must appear on the matter file.

8.5   Practices will ensure compliance with the requirements of the Solicitors' Costs Information and Client Care Code in relation to initial costs information and, in particular, the provision of the 'best information possible on the likely overall costs of the matter, including a breakdown between fees, VAT and disbursements' (4a). Where there are special circumstances making the provision of this information inappropriate, the special considerations must be noted on the matter file. In relation to standing agreed terms with regular clients see section 7.2.

8.6   Practices will ensure that the strategy for the matter is always apparent on the matter file and that in complex cases a separate case plan is developed. Save in exceptional cases the client must be consulted upon and kept informed of the strategy in the matter and any planned changes to it.

8.7   Practices will have documented procedures to ensure that matters are progressed in an appropriate manner. In particular:

    a: Key information must be recorded on the file.
    b: Key dates must be recorded on the file and in a back-up system.
    c: A timely response is made to telephone calls and correspondence from the client and others.
    d: Information on cost is provided at least every six months and, in publicly funded matters, the effect of the statutory charge, if any, is provided to the client in accordance with the Solicitors' Costs Information and Client Care Code.
    e: Clients are informed in writing if the person with conduct of their matter changes, or there is a change of person to whom any problem with service should be addressed.

8.8   Practices will document procedures for the giving, monitoring and discharge of undertakings.

8.9   Practices will have a documented procedure to:

    a: List open and closed matters, identify all matters for a single client and linked files where relevant and all files for particular funders.
    b: Ensure that they are able to identify and trace any documents, files, deeds, wills or any other items relating to a matter.
    c: Safeguard the confidentiality of matter files and all other client information.
    d: Ensure that the status of the matter and the action taken can be easily checked by other members of the practice.
    e: Ensure that documents are stored on the matter file(s) in an orderly way.

8.10   Practices will have a documented procedure for using barristers, expert witnesses and other external advisers who are involved in the delivery of legal services, which will include provision for the following:

    a: Use of clear selection criteria, which do not discriminate on grounds of race, colour, ethnic or national origins, sex, creed, disability, sexual orientation or age.
    b: Where appropriate, consultation with the client in relation to selection, and proper advice to the client on choice of advocate or other professional.
    c: Clients to be advised of the name and status of the person being instructed, how long she/he might take to respond, and where disbursements are to be paid by the client, the cost involved.
    d: Maintenance of records (centrally, by department or office) on barristers and experts used, including evidence of assessment against the criteria.
    e: Evaluation of performance, for the information of other members of the practice.
    f: Giving of instructions, which clearly describe what is required and which, in litigation matters, comply with the rules of court and any court orders.
    g: Checking of opinions and reports received to ensure they adequately provide the information sought (and, in litigation matters, comply with the rules of court and any court orders).
    h: Payment of fees.

8.11   Practices will have documented procedures to ensure that, at the end of the matter, the practice:

    a: Reports to the client on the outcome and explains any further action that the client is required to take in the matter and what (if anything) the practice will do.

b: Accounts to the client for any outstanding money.

c: Returns to the client any original documents or other property belonging to the client if required (save for items, which are by agreement to be stored by the practice).

d: If appropriate, advises the client about arrangements for storage and retrieval of papers and other items retained (in so far as this has not already been dealt with, for example in terms of business) and any charges to be made in this regard.

e: Advises the client whether they should review the matter in future and, if so, when and why.

f: Archives or destroys files in an appropriate manner.

V Assessment criteria

1 STRUCTURES AND POLICIES

Section 1 deals with a number of policies that practices will need to have in place. In some cases these duplicate Law Society requirements, but their inclusion in the Lexcel standard makes it clear that they are subject to assessment under the scheme. Other professional rules – most notably the Solicitors' Accounts Rules – do not form part of the standard and are not therefore subject to assessment under the Lexcel scheme.

In some cases there is a Law Society code which will be required to be in place, most obviously in the areas of equal opportunities and anti-discrimination. For private practice firms it is a breach of the regulations not to have adopted these policies, while employed practices are likely to be subject to organisation-wide policies. In other cases practices will need to address the requirements and decide the right approach for them.

Key issues

- Management structure.
- Business model.
- The role of quality in management.
- Responsibility for quality management.
- Reviews of the quality programme.
- Anti-discrimination.
- Equality of opportunity.
- Avoiding money laundering.
- Combating mortgage fraud.
- What is the most appropriate format for the necessary documentation? One document or a series of linked documents?
- Staff involvement in the preparation of policies covered in this section and communication and training thereafter.
- If and how to communicate relevant policies to clients and others that the practice deals with.

1.1 Practices will have documentation setting out the legal framework under which they operate.

For many practices this will be one of the most fundamental considerations – the basis on which the practice is formed. In the case of partnerships there is always the risk of a breakdown of working relationships or other difficulties between the members of the firm and it will be good practice to have a partnership deed, dealing with such issues as:

a: Management and voting rights.
b: The authorisation of individual partners or managers to bind the practice in contract.

c: Rights to share in profits.

d: How capital contributions will be dealt with and rights to interest.

e: How capital will be repaid.

f: Entry to and expulsions and retirements from the firm.

g: The rights of partners to elect part-time working patterns and provisions for parental leave, including maternity provisions.

h: The situation in case of long-term illness or incapacity.

i: How succession will be achieved, if appropriate.

j: Continuity of the practice in the event of death or incapacity in the case of small or sole practices.

Although a formal and binding deed is regarded as good practice, the actual format and detail of such documentation is for each practice to determine. Assessors will need to satisfy themselves that the issues covered above have received appropriate consideration.

Sole practitioners should consider leaving a letter or other instructions with a fellow practitioner, if there are reciprocal arrangements, or a friend or relative to deal with their wishes for the practice in the case of death or incapacity. It is also possible that the sole practitioner's will could deal with certain of the provisions above; a recommendation to this effect appears in *The Guide to the Professional Conduct of Solicitors 1999*.

It is recognised that the contents of any deed or other documentation are likely to be sensitive and confidential. Practices may choose to decline to disclose such documentation to assessors, in which case formal, written confirmation from the firm may be acceptable evidence of compliance. This might be supplemented by interview evidence from partners.

In the case of in-house departments the documentation should set out the relationship of the legal department to the parent body and any colleague departments. This could be done by reference to organisation-wide documents or charters, or any legislative provisions, public or private.

Example of major non-compliances

- There is no document setting out the legal framework under which the practice operates, and the size or composition of the practice would make it impracticable to address this within 21 days.

Example of minor non-compliances

- There is no statement of the legal framework under which the practice operates or it does not deal with the relevant issues sufficiently.

1.2   Consideration should be given to the most appropriate business structure and this should be kept under review as part of the business planning process (section 2).

Although the great majority of practices remain sole practices or traditional unlimited liability partnerships there have been considerable developments in other possible business structures. Firms have been able to incorporate themselves for some time and further details on this option can be obtained by contacting the Law Society ethics department. As of July 2002 there were 158 incorporated practices registered with the Law Society. Since April 2001 it has been possible to form as or convert into a limited liability partnership. Whereas in the ordinary unlimited liability partnership the partners all have joint and several liability for the debts of the firm, the contribution of each member of a limited liability partnership is limited to his or her share of the assets unless there is an agreement to the contrary. Outgoing partners can therefore also be fully relieved of liabilities that arise at a future date, such as from claims after they leave the firm relating to incidents while they were there.

Limited liability partnership status limits the liability of individual partners but does not limit the exposure of the firm. A separate consideration is therefore whether the firm should limit its liability in relation to all or some of instructions received. This is becoming increasingly common in commercial practices.

In-house practices in local authorities, other public sector bodies, and those in commerce and industry, are likely to provide evidence in the corporate plans of the umbrella organisation.

Example of major non-compliances

- Consideration has not been given to the most appropriate business structure for the practice, and the size or composition of the practice would make it impracticable to do this within 21 days.

Example of minor non-compliances

- There has been no review or adequate review of the structure.

1.3 Practices will have a risk management strategy or framework.

Example of major non-compliances

- There is no risk management strategy or framework documented, and it would be impracticable to address this within 21 days.

Example of minor non-compliances

- There is a risk management strategy or framework, but it is not comprehensive.

1.4 Practices will have a written quality policy. This is a high level document setting out the organisation's commitment to quality and overall policy. Practices will also have documented procedures as set out in this standard, which will be distributed and published throughout the practice showing:

a: The role that the quality system plays in the overall strategy of the practice.
b: Who has responsibility for the management of the quality system.

It is all too common for lawyers to see a quality management system as being a set of procedures that they have to follow. Section 1.4 requires there to be an overall policy – or management approach – to why the practice has adopted a quality management system. In-house practices are likely to be covered by an organisation-wide quality policy. It is important that the policy is not simply a formula of words devised by the partners or managers to satisfy this requirement. Assessors should seek evidence that people throughout the practice understand why a quality management system is in place, share a commitment to it and understand who should benefit from it.

Practices should consider publicising their quality policy, as by including it in client literature or any terms of business, or displaying it in reception areas used by clients, if appropriate.

In addition to the quality policy every practice will also have processes and documented procedures to address all the particular requirements for day-to-day compliance. These processes and procedures should be seen to be integral to making sense of the quality policy. There will need to be ongoing reviews of the effectiveness of the quality management system; consideration should always be given to whether current arrangements advance the quality policy within the practice.

Example of major non-compliances

- There is evidence of ignorance of the quality policy within the firm and the size or composition of the practice will make it impracticable to address this within 21 days.

Example of minor non-compliances

- There is no quality policy or there is insufficient evidence of its being understood within the practice.

1.5   There must be one designated individual who has particular responsibility for the quality system. Practices must be able to show that this individual has sufficient authority and seniority to raise concerns regarding the quality system and to have any such issues resolved.

It is recognised that responsibility for the management and operation of the quality system will be shared in most practices, but the requirements in 1.5 is that there should be one named individual who has the ultimate responsibility for the successful operation and development of quality in the practice. Where responsibility is shared consideration should be given to producing a quality organisation chart, and/or a statement of job roles and responsibilities and reporting lines.

Assessors will seek evidence that the person nominated as being the head of quality does have sufficient standing within the organisation to address problems and resolve them if possible. In local authorities, other public sector bodies, and those in commerce and industry, the designated individual with overall responsibility for quality in the organisation may be outside the practice. Assessors will seek evidence that an individual has responsibility for implementing the organisation's quality policy within the practice.

Example of minor non-compliances

- There is no designated individual who has responsibility for the quality system or there is evidence that such an appointee does not have sufficient seniority to meet the requirements of the role.

1.6   There must be a review of the operation of the quality system at least annually and a process for people within the practice to suggest improvements to the system. The review must show the part that the quality system is intended to play in the future strategy of the practice over the next 12 months at least.

If the quality system is to be a living system that develops within the practice, it will need regular reviews to see how it needs to be changed. The requirements in this provision are that, at least annually, the practice should be able to show a process whereby the system and its procedures have been considered and amended if and where appropriate. Reviewing complaints received (see 7.3) and clients' perceptions of services provided (see 7.4) provide a good starting point for a review of the quality system. In addition, many practices will seek input from the heads of departments or teams, which may be combined with a formal system of staff suggestions for improvements. In-house practices should be able to provide evidence that they have been gathering relevant data on the operation of the quality system within the department as well as participating in any organisation-wide quality reviews, if the latter are restricted to limited quality issues, such as response times. Such structures do not need to be documented as procedures, though in many cases practices are likely to choose to do so in order that the process is transparent within the practice.

Example of major non-compliances

- There is a process in place by which people within the practice can suggest improvements to the quality system, but there is insufficient evidence that it is in effective operation.

Example of minor non-compliances

- There has been no review or adequate review of the operation of the quality system within the previous 12 months where the system has been in place for at least that period of time.

1.7   Practices will document procedures on non-discrimination, and have regard to guidance from the Law Society on non-discrimination in accepting instructions from clients, the use of experts and counsel and the provision of services to clients.

All firms in private practice are required to adopt the model policy of the Law Society which is reviewed from time to time. In local authorities, other public sector bodies, and those in commerce and industry, practices may be subject to the policies of the umbrella organisation. Assessors will expect these to meet the above requirement except where a practice can demonstrate that they conflict with a statutory requirement or guidance from a statutory body, and that the practice meets those requirements. Whereas, formerly,

Lexcel assessors would only satisfy themselves that the necessary policy was in place and would not monitor whether the policy was in effective operation, they are now required to raise concerns based on interview evidence within the practice or other evidence emerging from the assessment that the policy is not being observed. For example, it may become clear that instructions are declined on grounds that suggest the documented policy is not being observed, or counsel or experts are excluded from authorised lists on unjustifiable grounds that may amount to discrimination contrary to the policy. It is recognised that this would amount to an allegation of a serious professional offence, so the procedure for this section (and the provisions in 1.8 on equality and diversity where similar considerations apply) is that the assessor should:

- Raise his or her concerns with the management representative during or at the end of the assessment, disclosing the evidence and its source if it has not been provided in confidence, such concerns to be noted sensitively in the main assessment report.
- Consider any response by the practice representative or allow him or her time to consider his or her response during the assessment or within the 21 days following the assessment.
- In cases of gross or serious failures of the policy which the assessor reasonably believes have not been addressed by the practice recommend all such concerns should be referred to the Lexcel office for further action.

Example of major non-compliances

- There is evidence of discrimination contrary to the required policy in relation to the provision of services, accepting instructions from clients, use of counsel or experts, or recruitment or employment practices.

Example of minor non-compliances

- The practice has not adopted the Law Society's policy on anti-discrimination or it cannot be produced.

1.8   Practices will document procedures on equality and diversity including recruitment and employment procedures and have regard to guidance on equality and diversity issued by the Law Society from time to time.

The implementation of this provision is subject to the same considerations as with non-discrimination in 1.7 above and the procedures by which assessors should raise and report concerns are also as stated in that section above. Examples could include that the practice has been found to have discriminated against a member of staff by an employment tribunal, or a member of staff may raise issues of discrimination or harassment.

Practices are also encouraged to seek additional guidance from the following organisations:

- Equal Opportunities Commission (**www.eoc.uk**)
- Advisory, Conciliation and Arbitration Service – ACAS (**www.acas.org.uk**)
- Commission for Racial Equality (**www.cre.gov.uk**)
- Disability Rights Commission (**www.drc-gb.org**)

Example of major non-compliances

- There is evidence that procedures on equality and diversity are not being adhered to, and therefore are not in effective operation.

Example of minor non-compliances

- The practice has not adopted the Law Society's policy on anti-discrimination or it cannot be produced.

1.9   Practices will have documented procedures to ensure compliance with money laundering legislation. The documented procedures should cover:

a: The appointment of a 'Nominated Officer', usually referred to as a Money Laundering Reporting Officer (MLRO).
b: Reporting of suspicious circumstances within the practice and by the MLRO to the authorities.
c: Identification checking.
d: Partner and staff training in anti-money laundering awareness.
e: The proper maintenance of records.

Any exemptions to these requirements must be stated in the practice's documented procedures.

The extension of the anti-money laundering regime to all 'criminal conduct' where there is 'criminal property' under the Proceeds of Crime Act 2002 has received extensive consideration in the legal press. Certain provisions under the Terrorism Act 2000 are also involved. The provisions of the Money Laundering Regulations 2003 are mandatory for most firms in private practice and it is a criminal offence not to have implemented the necessary provisions, regardless of whether money laundering is actually occurring within the firm.

Local authorities, other public sector bodies, and those in commerce and industry, will need to consider whether and if so, how, these provisions apply to them.

The implementation of the Money Laundering Regulations 2003 will need to be in line with current Law Society guidance. Practices should bear in mind that sections 330 and 331 of the Proceeds of Crime Act 2002 provide that in deciding whether a person has committed an offence of failure to report 'the court must consider whether he followed any relevant guidance which was at the time … issued by the supervisory authority or any other competent authority'. Since the Law Society is within this range of organisations the fact that professional guidance has been followed may well provide an effective defence to a prosecution.

Example of major non-compliances

- The practice has not addressed some or all of the requirements of the Money Laundering Regulations 2003 where they apply, or the procedures are used so inconsistently that they could not be said to be in effective operation.

Example of minor non-compliances

- Procedures dealing with the avoidance of money laundering liability are not documented where required, although they are in operation, or documented procedures do not address one or more of the areas that are required to be covered.

1.10   Practices providing services to clients in relation to property transactions will have documented procedures in relation to the avoidance of involvement in mortgage fraud.

Private practice firms providing conveyancing services will need to have clear guidelines in relation to procedures to be followed in the event of suspicions of mortgage fraud. The requirements of the *Council of Mortgage Lenders Handbook* will also be a concern for most firms providing conveyancing services.

Full guidance on avoiding mortgage fraud can be obtained by contacting the Law Society Ethics Department.

Example of major non-compliances

- There are no procedures for avoiding mortgage fraud in a practice that provides conveyancing services to purchasers or the procedures are so poorly observed that they are not in effective operation.

Example of minor non-compliances

- Procedures for avoiding mortgage fraud are not documented in a practice that provides conveyancing services to purchasers, although they are in operation, or the documented procedures do not address one or more of the areas that are required to be covered.

1.11   Practices will have a documented policy in relation to data protection compliance issues.

In 2002 Elizabeth France – the then outgoing Information Commissioner – revealed that only some 25% of law firms in private practice had registered under the Data Protection Act 1998. A more active regime of enforcing the need to register and observe the data protection principles was announced.

Registration with the Information Commissioner's Office, where it is necessary to do so, commits the organisation to the data protection principles and the necessary internal controls that will be needed. Practices must register if they record and process data that identifies an individual, which includes any expression of opinion.

Example of major non-compliances

- There is no policy in relation to data protection compliance or the policy is so poorly observed that it is not in effective operation.

Example of minor non-compliances

- The policy in relation to data protection compliance is not documented, although it is in operation, or it does not address one or more of the areas that are required to be covered.

1.12 Practices will have a documented policy in relation to the health and safety of partners, staff and visitors to the practice.

There are general duties on employers and organisations to ensure a safe working environment. In accordance with the applicable legislation, practices should adopt a policy that they are taking adequate steps to ensure that they meet their obligations. More detailed procedures on this point appear at 4.2.

Example of major non-compliances

- There is no policy in relation to health and safety or the policy is so poorly observed that it is not in effective operation.

Example of minor non-compliances

- The policy in relation to health and safety is not documented or does not address one or more of the areas that are required to be covered.

2 STRATEGY, THE PROVISION OF SERVICES AND MARKETING

Section 2 deals with the need for a business plan and for due consideration to be given to marketing. Underlying these provisions is a requirement that Lexcel awarded practices need to consider effective strategies in order to remain successful.

Private practice firms might choose one all-embracing document for these requirements or the plans could be broken into a series of departmental plans. All will depend on the style, size and culture of the practice. The in-house practice might need to refer to organisation-wide plans, perhaps supplemented by further details on planning within the department.

Whatever the choices made, it is a requirement that plans are committed to some form of documentation. If this is not made available to the assessors some other evidence of its existence and adequacy will be needed.

Key issues

- Format of business and marketing plans.
- In private practice, the aspirations of the partners.
- Realistic objectives for the practice.
- Scope of research of internal and external factors.
- Extent of staff involvement in compilation of plans.
- Extent to which plans are shared with and communicated to staff.
- What marketing would be appropriate and what is intended from it.

2.1   Practices will develop and maintain a marketing and a business plan.

A business plan should consist of:

a: Analysis of the factors, both internal to the practice and externally, that are relevant to the future development of the practice.
b: Key objectives for the forthcoming 12 months at least from the date of the document or review of any such document to provide a background against which the practice may measure its performance.
c: Some outline or detailed objectives covering a further two years at least which evidence a consideration of the factors relevant to the future of the practice.
d: For items (b) and (c) above a finance plan, evidencing due consideration of the overall financial implications of the strategy or strategies to be adopted within the practice and setting some financial goals or objectives if not appearing elsewhere in the business plan.

Some form of strategic document or business plan is required by this provision. In some practices this may be achieved through a combination of different documents – perhaps a main business plan for the firm along with a series of departmental plans. In local authority and in-house practices, the assessor would expect to see a service plan or documented references to the corporate plans of the umbrella organisation. The assessor will expect the practice to have documented what it seeks to achieve, within the limits imposed by corporate or statutory prescription. It is for each practice to choose the format and style of the documentation. It follows that the length and complexity of the documentation will vary between similar practices.

Factors that will determine the complexity of the strategic documentation will include:

- The size of the practice – sole practices and smaller firms will often have simpler strategies and less need for complex documentation.
- The amount of change that is anticipated over the period of the plan – a practice seeking to consolidate or stabilise its current operations will probably have less to address than one that is expanding.
- The management style of the partners or managers.
- The organisational requirements in local authorities or other in-house departments.

Whatever the style and format of the documentation, assessors will seek evidence of analysis of significant factors – both internal and external to the practice – which will be likely to have an impact on the future of the practice. This analysis could take various forms, but could include:

- staff survey;
- internal 'brainstorming' sessions;
- assessment within the practice of 'SWOT' factors (strengths, weaknesses, opportunities and threats);
- consideration of proposed legislative changes or Government plans;
- consultation of local plans;
- organisation-wide plans for in-house departments.

Performance objectives are intended to provide hard data as to whether the plan has succeeded or not. Wherever possible, objectives should be 'smart', i.e.:

        Specific

        Measurable

        Achievable

        Realistic

        Time-limited

Objectives may relate to gross fee income, size of the organisation, or any performance ratios felt to be relevant, including client satisfaction.

The standard recognises that objectives for the current or next 12 months should in most cases be more detailed than those for the medium-term future.

It is a requirement that the financial implications of the strategy are shown to have been considered. This will result either in evidence being available of such consideration or the establishment of financial objectives within the business or departmental plans. A finance plan is best seen as a management overview of the financial implications of the strategy in question. It is separate from, but perhaps ancillary to, more detailed budgets.

However marketing is dealt with, the documentation should cover:

a: Areas of work that the practice wishes to develop, expand, reduce or cease to provide.
b: The benefits that the practice hopes to achieve from its marketing or promotional activity.
c: Any promotional methods that will be employed and responsibility for them.
d: A budget for promotional activities.

The standard does not require all recognised practices to market themselves actively – merely that they should consider the appropriate marketing activity for the practice. The practice content with its current supply of work, or which feels that instructions may need to be turned away because of excess demand, would not be expected to involve itself in promotion that is likely to further increase the flow of potential instructions. If a decision is made not to engage in active marketing, it must be documented in order to meet this requirement. On the other hand, a practice that sets out in its main strategy a desire to develop all or some of its practice areas would need to show that the marketing steps that will be needed have been considered.

Example of major non-compliances

- There is no marketing and/or business plan and the size or composition of the practice would make it impracticable to address this within 21 days.

Examples of minor non-compliances

- There is no marketing documentation available at the assessment when it is clear that marketing activity is undertaken by the practice.
- There is some shortcoming in the documentation which is available at the assessment, such as:
  - Lack of evidence of analysis of relevant factors to inform the business plan.
  - No objectives or objectives which are too vague for the practice to measure its performance at some future stage.
  - Inadequate consideration of the financial implications of the strategy or strategies described.

2.2   Practices will document the services they wish to offer, the client groups to be served, how services are to be provided (including any special features) and the way in which services are designed to meet client needs.

It is important that the practice should consider and record the extent or scope of its services and also any limitations to them. This will be useful to:

- clients wishing to check if the practice can deal with their concerns;
- other external persons such as referrers of work;
- staff, as on induction training.

Since, in most cases, it will be clients and potential clients who have most interest in this provision, the requirements will often be met by lists and details of services as contained in brochures or on websites.

The sort of special features which will commonly be listed will be the languages that advice can be offered through, the availability of home visits, wheelchair access to the offices, etc.

Practices providing publicly funded services should list the contract categories that are offered and any policy established on the acceptance of instructions given any limitations to matter starts.

Local authority departments might describe or append service agreements with colleague departments, or external authorities that are advised through contractual arrangements.

Example of major non-compliances

- The practice has not considered or documented any of the requirements of 2.2, and the size or composition of the practice would make it impracticable to address this within 21 days.

Example of minor non-compliances

- No list of services is available or some element (e.g. special features, when provided) is missing.

2.3 The documents required by section 2.1 must be reviewed every six months and the review must be documented. The services and marketing plan or documentation required by section 2.2 must be produced or reviewed at least annually and must be current at the time of any assessment.

Practices must be able to show that all strategic and marketing documentation is kept under continual review. There will need to be a substantive review at least annually and an interim review at least six-monthly. The evidence of such reviews could be partnership strategy papers or partnership or management group minutes. Sole practitioners must also be able to demonstrate that reviews have taken place as required, for example by way of dated notes or appendices to plans.

Issues for practices

- Type, length and style of desired documentation.
- Possible involvement of external advice.
- Staff involvement and communication to the staff.
- Feasible marketing activity and its budget.
- Most effective format of review.

Assessment guidelines

Plans which are shortly to come into operation or which are already implemented for the current 12 months will be acceptable.

It is not a requirement of the standard that staff must be consulted on and informed of the business plan or other documentation described in this section. It is, however, increasingly regarded as good business practice to involve staff in the business planning process and to keep them informed of the practice's plans and progress.

The contents of all business or marketing plans can be retained as being confidential to the practice, if it so chooses. In such circumstances the assessor will seek evidence of the existence and understanding of such plans from interviews. Interviews are likely to be at partner or senior manager level as these are the people most likely to be involved in business strategy.

Example of major non-compliances

- No reviews have taken place.

Example of minor non-compliances

- A review has taken place but it has not been documented.

3 FINANCIAL MANAGEMENT

This section requires there to be clear management responsibility for financial management and various controls to monitor the use of available funds and, in the case of private practice, business performance.

It is recognised that many in-house departments will not need to set the targets and to monitor performance as required by this section. Local authority and other public institution practices should consider, however, any recharge arrangements and their application to legal work performed within the department. Where services are provided to authorities on a contracted out basis many of the controls associated with private practice become appropriate.

Key issues

- Responsibility for financial controls and performance.
- Preparation of financial reports and future budgets.
- Responsibility for monitoring performance against budgets.
- Time recording within the practice: when it is required and who undertakes it.

3.1 Practices will document responsibility for financial management procedures.

In an increasing number of private practice firms it may be an employee who has responsibility for monitoring and correcting financial performance issues, or it may be shared responsibility between an employee and the partners or a finance or managing partner.

There is no requirement as to the seniority of the person or persons concerned.

In the local authority practice responsibility for financial performance may lie outside the department, e.g. a designated contact in the finance department.

Example of major non-compliances

- There are no documented procedure and staff are unclear about who is responsible for financial management.

Example of minor non-compliances

- Nobody has been designated as having responsibility for financial management or it is not clear from the documentation available or interviews within the practice who has such responsibility.

3.2 Practices will be able to provide documentary evidence of their financial management processes, including:

a: Annual budget (including, where appropriate, any capital expenditure proposed).
b: Variance analysis conducted at least quarterly of income and expenditure against budgets.

c: Annual profit and loss or income and expenditure accounts (certificated or audited accounts).

d: Annual balance sheet.

e: Annual cash or funds flow forecast.

f: Quarterly variance analysis at least of cashflow.

Financial management data is best evidenced by showing all appropriate data or paperwork to assessors, but practices may decline to do so if they wish. In such cases the assessors will consider other evidence that is available, including correspondence from the practice's auditor and interviews with the partners and/or managers.

In private practice the production of a profit and loss account and a balance sheet are commonplace. Firms could often improve, however, in the area of management accounting, i.e. planning for future performance rather than reporting on the past.

Assessors will take into account that many firms will not necessarily engage their auditors to advise on management accounting issues. They should therefore enquire as to the extent of the accountants' involvement in the firm in considering any assurance from such advisers that the requirements of this section have been addressed.

Example of major non-compliances

- There is no system of establishing and undertaking variance analysis of future budgets or income and/or expenditure in circumstances where they could fairly be excluded (e.g. local authority department where financial matters are controlled outside the legal department).

Example of minor non-compliances

- One or more of the elements of 3.2 are not evident and/or a quarterly variance analysis of a budget or cash flow statement is overdue.

3.3   Practices will have a time recording process which enables the accurate measurement of time spent on matters for billing purposes and/or management analysis of the cost effectiveness of work and the efficiency of the practice.

Computerised time recording has become the norm for most types of legal practice in recent years. It is not compulsory that any such system is computerised: in some smaller firms file-based or manual systems are still in use and this will be acceptable.

Most private practitioners see time recording as a matter of collecting billing data and therefore decline to record non-chargeable time. Likewise, many in-house lawyers or those in private practice working to fixed fees will not time-record. In non-private practice, time recording and billing systems may not be linked as billing is governed by inter-departmental agreements. The provision in 3.3 reflects the growing view that time recording should be seen as management data first and billing information second. It is nonetheless acceptable that a practice could take the view that it will only time-record on those matters that will need to be billed or costed on a time recorded basis (if any) and decline to time-record elsewhere. Where some matters or types of matter are not normally subject to time recording, practices may wish to carry out a time recording exercise on a sample basis. This would provide a benchmark to ensure that fixed fee or percentage-based fees are viable.

Example of major non-compliances

- There is no system of time recording where time is nonetheless a factor in charges to clients (or client departments in employed practice).

Example of minor non-compliances

- There is a system of time recording in existence but one or more fee-earners who are required to record time in this way is or are not doing so. However, if the assessor identifies extensive non-compliance with a time recording system, to the extent that the system could not be said to be in effective operation, that could amount to a major non-compliance.

4 FACILITIES AND INFORMATION TECHNOLOGY

Lawyers have always required office premises and related facilities from which to operate. More recently the importance and use of computers has become a major consideration for all practices. Of equal concern is the growing volume of compliance requirements in relation to data control and computer use.

In-house lawyers may be subject to organisation-wide policies and procedures in relation to all or most of this section of the standard.

Key issues

- The needs of the firm and all its personnel in relation to office accommodation, having regard to:

  - The importance of a comfortable and secure working environment.
  - Health and safety responsibilities.
  - The projection of an appropriate image to clients.
  - The maintenance of effective 'back-office' services.

- Maintaining client confidentiality and providing an effective service through computer communication systems.
- Compliance with requirements in relation to e-mail use and storage, data protection registrations and any related requirements of the firm's insurers.
- What the firm would do should a catastrophic event occur – e.g. the office is burned: business continuity plan.

4.1   Practices will document the office facilities needed to provide a service to clients, including:

a: The use of premises and equipment, including security and related health and safety issues.
b: Photocopying, including maintenance and support.
c: Arrangements for clients to visit the offices, including reception, directions and car parking, if appropriate.
d: Staff facilities.
e: Mail, fax and other communication arrangements.
f: Procedures for the handling of financial transactions.

Some practices may choose to address these requirements through one document, while others may comply with a series of documents, whether co-ordinated or not. Practices may choose the style and complexity of documentation that suits them best, but in most cases these provisions will be set out in the practice's office procedures manual. It is important that the arrangements required above should be accessible to all personnel within the practice.

Practices are required to have a policy on health and safety (1.12) which must be subject to at least an annual review (4.2). The sort of arrangements that might additionally be documented under this section might include how and when risk assessments are conducted, arrangements for eye tests for screen users, fire drills, testing of fire extinguishers, etc.

Many practices will have arrangements in place on the maintenance of photocopying equipment and contractual arrangements for external copying of large or multiple copies. Computer support contracts become increasingly significant as more work is entrusted to data format or conducted via e-mails.

The importance of client reactions to the offices has often been stressed. The state of the reception area, the professionalism of the welcome and the availability of refreshments should be seen as an important element of the client care policy of the practice. Issues to be addressed might include:

- How clients will be informed of delays.
- How and when refreshments will be offered and served.
- The provision of up-to-date magazines, newspapers and publicity matter on the firm.
- Ensuring that floral displays are kept fresh.

In most firms the provision of confidential facilities for clients who need to have documents signed or other short communications within the reception area should be considered. In too many practices confidential information will be overheard by other clients awaiting an appointment.

The efficient use of communication facilities might require training for those personnel concerned, for example, familiarisation with the features of the practice's telephone system is likely to form part of induction.

In most practices the accounts procedures will be a significant element of the overall practice manual and should provide worked examples of entries for payments in, cheque payments, payments of petty cash, transfers, etc. Breaches of the Solicitors' Accounts Rules are a significant risk for firms in private practice and the availability of clear instructions forms an effective safeguard in this respect and can assist in minimising wasted time between accounts and fee-earning personnel.

Examples of major non-compliances

- There is no documentation dealing with office facilities or it fails to address most or all of the issues.
- There is evidence of widespread ignorance of the facilities dealt with under 4.1 or of a significant amount or aspect of them.

Examples of minor non-compliances

- Documentation does exist in relation to office facilities but it fails to deal with a limited number of the issues referred to or fails to do so adequately.
- There is evidence that staff are not fully aware of relevant facilities or processes covered by 4.1.
- There is evidence that the documented procedures are not being followed, to a limited extent.

4.2   Practices will conduct a documented review of health and safety issues at least annually. They must show that it has received due consideration by top management and implementation has been acted upon or is planned, as appropriate.

There is a requirement in the Health and Safety at Work Act 1974 for an annual review of health and safety in all organisations employing five persons or more. The review might form part of an annual review of the business plan or be one element of the annual review of all risk assessment data (see 6.7f). Sole and small practices which may not be caught by the legislation must still comply with this requirement although it is likely that the documentation they produce will be relatively short and straightforward. Practices can choose the degree of detail that they work into such a review. However, the report must show a genuine consideration of the principal issues affecting health and safety in professional offices, to include:

- Equipment.
- Safe handling and use of substances.
- Information, instruction and supervision on health and safety issues.
- Any training required.
- Accidents, first aid and work-related ill-health.
- Monitoring of conditions and systems of work.
- Emergency procedures, fire and evacuation of premises.

Examples of major non-compliances

- There has been no review of health and safety within the previous 12 months and the size of the practice makes such a review unlikely within the period of 21 days.
- There is no evidence that top management has considered any review and/or there is a failure to implement or plan to act upon its findings.

Example of minor non-compliances

- The annual review has taken place but is not documented.

4.3   There should be a business continuity plan envisaging the nature of catastrophic events that could beset the practice and the contingency plans that should be put into effect should they become necessary.

The need for business continuity planning arises from the practice's responsibilities to its clients and the need to comply with requirements imposed by legislation, practice rules and insurers. An increasing number of indemnity insurers are insisting upon the existence of a recently reviewed business continuity plan as a condition of insurance.

The business continuity plan should address the following issues:

a: An analysis of the practice's information technology systems required both to enable it to function and to deliver its advertised services to clients.
b: An analysis of the data it holds relating to: the practice; its personnel; its clients and business partners.

c: A description of the facilities and information technology systems it has in place for the storage and retrieval of data in the event of a disaster that prevents the operational activities of the practice.

d: Procedures for the identification and location of key personnel whose services will be available in the event of disaster and training and education in respect of their responsibilities.

e: The availability of 'standby systems' as a temporary measure in the event of disaster; or, where a decision is taken to outsource business continuity planning strategies to a managed or application service provider, evidence that proper consideration has been given to: selection of an appropriate provider; the contract of service; the cost; compliance with the Data Protection Act 1998; and the resolution of disputes.

Example of major non-compliances

- There is no business continuity plan in existence.

Example of minor non-compliances

- During interviews it becomes apparent that a limited number of staff are not aware of the business continuity plan.

4.4   Practices will have a plan for IT use setting out the use of IT facilities within the practice and any planned changes. The IT plan should cover:

   a: Responsibility for IT purchasing, installation, maintenance, support and training.
   b: The current and planned applications within the practice of IT.
   c: A data protection compliance statement in relation to staff, clients and others and registration with the Information Commissioner.
   d: Compliance with all appropriate regulations and requirements.
   e: User safety (see also 4.2 above).
   f: Appropriate use of e-mail and attachments, both externally and internally, including storage of messages and the implications of not observing such procedures.
   g: Computer data and system back up, to the extent not covered in any disaster recovery plan.

   The IT plan must address at least a period of the current or next 12 months and may form part of the practice's overall strategy documentation, the office manual, or a separate document.

Practices must demonstrate a regular review of the use and development of information technology systems. This does not require a particular level of computerisation and assessors will not judge the appropriateness of the information technology plan. They will, however, need to be satisfied that the use of information technology for delivering the practice's services has received due consideration by partners or managers. Each practice must decide how to address the issues set out in this section.

In section 4.4f (e-mail), a policy should specify: suitable business use; suitable personal use; the legal implications of e-mail (e.g. defamation and harassment); security issues and standards (e.g. viruses and 'spam' communications); criteria for the use of e-mail notices (e.g. disclaimers, etc.); whether the practice will accept service electronically; and procedures for electronic storage of e-mail.

A policy regarding use of the internet should specify: the general policy of the practice; suitable business use; suitable personal use; the legal implications of using the internet (e.g. downloading copyright or obscene material); and security standards.

A policy regarding the practice website should specify the practice's policy on: the management of site content (e.g. facilities for disabled users); the use of disclaimers; jurisdiction and applicable law in respect of site content; linking to other sites; copyright issues; and privacy of data collected from site visitors. Practices may wish to consider applying to the Legal Services Commission for its 'Quality Mark for Websites'.

A policy regarding electronic legal services should specify: the key legal, regulatory, professional and codified provisions to be observed; the procedures to be observed for on-line contracting; and the method of handling of electronic payments.

In section 4.4c (data management), a policy should specify: the different types of data that will be collected; the need for compliance with the eight data protection principles of the Data Protection Act 1998; and the assignment of responsibility for training and implementation.

In section 4.4d (legal and regulatory compliance), practices will need to ensure that at least one member of senior management has a working knowledge and understanding of the application of provisions with compliance implications for the practice's use of information technology and internet technologies. Further details are contained in the *Office Procedures Manual*.

Examples of major non-compliances

- The firm's website does not supply the information specified by the E-commerce (EC Directive) Regulations 2002.
- The firm has not notified itself as a 'data controller' under the Data Protection Act 1998.
- There is no documentation dealing with the use of information technology or it fails to address most or all of the issues referred to.

Example of minor non-compliances

- There is an IT plan but one or more of the elements that should be covered have not been addressed or have not been addressed adequately.

4.5   Practices will document arrangements for legal research and library facilities, whether in the practice or externally and whether through books or periodicals or computer-based services. A process must exist for the updating and sharing of legal and professional information.

This provision does not require the practice to have its own law library, though many do. What is important is that fee-earners have reasonable access to legal research tools, which in many practices will increasingly be web-based. There should be reasonable controls regarding location of reports, books, periodicals and other journals, along with distribution arrangements for updating material if appropriate.

The reference to knowledge management means that consideration needs to be given to the sharing of know-how, be it notes of research from within the firm, materials from courses attended, discussions at team or departmental meetings, counsels' opinions that might be of general interest within the practice, the accessibility of precedents and also, subject to data protection principles, client information as in a marketing database.

Example of major non-compliances

- There are no legal research or library facilities.

Example of minor non-compliances

- Arrangements for library and research facilities do exist but are not documented.
- Arrangements for library and research facilities do exist but fail to meet relevant needs, for example they do not cover certain areas of the practice, or are not fully up to date.

4.6   Practices will maintain an office manual collating information on office practice, which must be available to all members of the practice. Practices will document their arrangements to:

   a: Note each page with the date and/or issue.
   b: Review the manual at least annually.
   c: Update the manual and record the date of amendments.

5 PEOPLE MANAGEMENT

The observation is commonly made that legal service providers are 'people businesses'. It follows that compliance with section 5 on arrangements for the management of personnel will be important to any plan to improve performance within the practice.

Section 5 concentrates on the devices needed for effective management and control of staff. Certain provisions extend to partners in the case of private practice, particularly job descriptions and appraisals which previously extended to employed staff only.

Assessors are now more specifically required to examine the effectiveness of arrangements in relation to people management than was the case under previous versions of the Lexcel standard.

Key issues

- Responsibility for developing and maintaining an effective personnel policy for the firm, in particular:
  - Who is responsible for recruitment.
  - Who drafts any job descriptions or other such documentation and who is required to approve it.
  - Who conducts induction training.
  - What should go onto a personnel file for each person within the practice and who should have access to it, taking into account the rights of employees as data subjects.
  - Who co-ordinates performance appraisals.
  - Who is responsible for training and who controls the budget.
  - Who checks for compliance with annual CPD requirements.

5.1 Practices will have a plan for the recruitment, development and welfare of their personnel, including:

> **a: Likely recruitment needs, whether for the practice as a whole, its departments or offices, which may form part of the practice's overall business plan or departmental or other operational plans.**
> **b: Training and development.**
> **c: Welfare and entitlements.**

The requirement in 5.1 is that practices should set out in their strategic documentation their plans for the recruitment, development and treatment of partners, managers and staff.

For guidance on the formulation of a recruitment plan see the *Lexcel Office Procedures Manual*.

The standard recognises that practices will have different ways of addressing the planning required by this provision. Some practices may include personnel requirements as a heading or part of a general business plan; others may have a separate 'staff plan'; or it may fall to heads of department or team leaders to address their requirements in operational plans for which they are responsible.

The length and complexity of the plan or plans will be for each practice to determine. However, assessors will want to see sufficient evidence of the issues raised by this provision receiving adequate consideration. A sole practitioner or small practice may have no plans to recruit staff. Where such is the case, a record of the decision must be made in order to satisfy requirement 5.1a.

The plan(s) will be confidential to the practice and need not be disclosed to the assessor. Practices that decline to show the documentation to assessors will have to convince them by other means that the personnel plan does exist and covers the necessary areas for compliance.

Good communication is an essential ingredient of management. The responsibility to foster it lies with partners, supervisors and line managers. A practice which satisfies this requirement will have taken steps to develop team spirit and will achieve greater efficiency through regular communication involving all members of the practice. Briefing arrangements may be of a formal or informal nature, including, for example, staff meetings, intranet and e-mail. The assessor will examine how effectively these communication processes operate by interviewing a cross-section of staff. Communications processes should be two-way and the assessor should look for evidence of this.

Non-private practices will need to demonstrate that staff are kept informed of any issues within the wider corporate body that affect them directly as well as its overall policies.

Where a sole practitioner practises without any staff, requirement 5.1b only applies to the sole practitioner and 5.1c does not apply.

Examples of major non-compliances

- There is no plan (documented or otherwise) covering the areas required by this section.
- The plan has not been put into effect.

Examples of minor non-compliances

- There is a documented plan covering most of the issues addressed by this section but one or more elements is missing or dealt with inadequately.
- The practice has arrangements dealing with the requirements of this section but they are not documented.
- Some limited elements of the plan have not been implemented.

5.2   Practices will list the tasks to be undertaken by all personnel within the practice – including partners – and document the skills, knowledge and experience required for individuals to fulfil their role satisfactorily, usually in the form of a person specification and job description.

All personnel within the practice – including partners – will need to have a job description or other such documentation in place. This requirement applies equally to sole practitioners. The precise format of the job documentation will be at the discretion of the practice, but typically should recite the job title and then cover the jobholder's place in the organisation, reporting lines, the main purpose(s) of the role and a list of specific responsibilities.

It is good practice to review the job description regularly; many practices do so at each appraisal meeting.

An assessor may request to see the job description of any individual within the practice.

Example of major non-compliances

- There are no job descriptions/person specifications for personnel within the practice or a substantial number of them do not exist.

Examples of minor non-compliances

- There are job descriptions/person specifications for most personnel within the practice but there is a limited number of personnel who do not have such documentation in place.
- A number of job descriptions do not bear sufficient resemblance to the duties of the jobholder and are in clear need of amendment or redrafting.

5.3   Practices will have procedures to deal effectively with recruitment into the practice, including:

    a: The identification of vacancies.
    b: The drafting of consequential job documentation, usually in the form of a job description.
    c: Methods of attracting candidates and applicants.
    d: Selection methods used.
    e: Storage of interview notes.
    f: Provision of information by way of feedback to unsuccessful candidates.
    g: Any use of medical examination and/or references.
    h: Confirmation of job offers.
    i: Maintenance of communication during the pre-joining period and starting instructions.

Effective recruitment into the practice will clearly make a substantial contribution to the quality of service by the organisation. It is an increasing trend that recruitment and selection are open processes which are seen to be as objective and non-discriminatory as possible.

Practices should ensure that the responsibility for recruitment is documented; in many firms there are different arrangements for the recruitment and selection of professional staff, secretaries and trainees.

There is no requirement that firms should necessarily employ techniques such as psychometric testing in personnel selection, take up references or conduct medical tests, but if they do the arrangements will need to be documented.

Practices should always maintain records of interview notes, not least so that any later claim of unfairness in the process can be rebutted or defended. The Data Protection Employment Practices Code (part 1) provides that interview notes should not be kept for longer than a year.

Example of major non-compliances

- There are no procedures for recruitment and selection or they are clearly inadequate in some material regard, for example practising certificates and professional standing are not checked when recruiting solicitors.

Examples of minor non-compliances

- There are procedures covering most of the issues addressed by this section but one or more elements are missing or are dealt with inadequately.
- There is a limited number of instances when the procedures have not been observed.

5.4   Practices will conduct an appropriate induction process to cover:

    a: The practice's aims.
    b: Management structure and the individual's job responsibilities.
    c: Terms and conditions of employment, personal and banking details for personnel records.
    d: Initial and future training requirements.
    e: Key policies, including equality and diversity and client care and office procedures.

It is recognised that the full induction process may be staggered over a period of time and may consist of the provision of reading materials, face-to-face meetings or the use of interactive materials on the firm's intranet. There is no need for a documented procedure setting out how induction training is provided, but assessors will need to see sufficient evidence that the induction process does cover the areas listed and is in effective operation.

Practices will need to ensure that personal details are taken at an early stage of the jobholder's time with the practice. These would typically cover banking details, next-of-kin and any medical condition.

Example of major non-compliances

- There is no induction training process or there is evidence that it is not in effective operation.

Examples of minor non-compliances

- There is an induction training process but a limited number of people who should have received induction training have not done so.
- Induction training has occurred as required but did not cover relevant topics.

5.5   The induction process must occur within a reasonable period of time of taking up the role.

In many firms there may be an initial induction meeting to be followed by more substantive induction training at a later date. It is important, however, that the new joiner is brought up to speed with his or her role as soon as practicable. Undue delays in doing so will limit the new joiner's effectiveness for the practice and may cause anxiety for the person concerned.

Example of minor non-compliances

- There is an induction training process but a limited number of people who should have received induction training have not done so within a reasonable time frame.

5.6   Appropriate induction processes must apply when existing personnel transfer roles within the practice.

Assessors will not necessarily expect the same degree of induction training for those transferring roles within the firm. The practice should examine which areas of the new role will need explanation and training, and may rely on earlier training or experience for more familiar elements.

Example of major non-compliances

- There is no induction training process for people who transfer roles within the practice.

Example of minor non-compliances

- There is an induction training process but a limited number of people who have transferred roles within the previous 12 months have not received induction training.

5.7   Practices will operate a process for:

   a: An annual review at least of responsibilities, objectives and performance for all partners and staff members.
   b: Written appraisal records, which will be confidential to the jobholder and named persons under the practice's data protection policy and may be inspected as evidence of compliance only with the consent of the jobholder.
   c: An annual review at least of the training and development needs of all personnel within the practice, recorded in an individual training and development plan.

An effective appraisal scheme is core to the performance management programme of most organisations. This does not necessarily mean, however, that the same documentation should be in use for all personnel or that the process should be unduly bureaucratic. Partner schemes, in particular, may be subject to quite different arrangements from the staff scheme or schemes.

The requirement in this section for written records and documented procedures is to ensure that difficult issues are addressed and that there is a written record of the discussions and agreements emerging from the process.

In most practices the setting of objectives will coincide with the annual appraisal meeting, but it does not necessarily have to. It is commonplace for financial objectives emerging from the budget, for example, to be settled before the start of the financial year and then reviewed in the appraisal meeting or even at ongoing departmental or office meetings.

Sole practitioners will need to review and document their own responsibilities and objectives.

It is good practice to review the individual's job description in an appraisal meeting, but it is not essential to do so.

Practices need not use the term 'appraisal' at all as long as they have procedures that meet the specified requirements. Some use terms such as 'performance review' or 'development review'. There is no standard appraisal scheme, but for sample forms see the *Office Procedures Manual* which contains a range of possible paperwork for adoption by practices. The publication also includes further guidance on the conduct of appraisal interviews.

Appraisal records are sensitive and will need to be subject to controls under data protection compliance considerations. The practice should make clear who has access to records and for how long they are retained. Assessors may only examine appraisal records with the express consent of the jobholder in question.

It is common practice to review training needs for jobholders within the appraisal meeting, perhaps in conjunction with other training reviews throughout the year. The appraisal process can therefore generate a training plan, whether on an organisation-wide, or departmental level. Sole practitioners need to document their own individual training and development plans.

Examples of major non-compliances

- There is no process for the setting of objectives and responsibilities and/or performance appraisal.
- There are no substantive records of appraisal meetings.
- There is no process whereby training and development needs are reviewed and planned.
- The processes that are adopted by the practice are clearly and materially ineffective, for example, because they have not been implemented in relation to a significant number of partners or staff.

Example of minor non-compliances

- There are systems for all the elements required by this section but in a limited number of instances these have not been followed.

5.8   Practices will ensure that appropriate training is provided to personnel within the practice in accordance with its policy on training and development. Training may be arranged on an in-house or external basis and may be on-line or through more traditional means. Where appropriate the training should be recognised for CPD purposes under the scheme operated by the Law Society of England and Wales or other professional bodies.

Training will typically be heavily linked to the appraisal scheme.

Assessors will seek evidence that:

a: Training needs are being assessed in an appropriate manner.
b: Agreed training needs are being provided for.
c: The effectiveness of training activity is monitored, and that unmet needs are addressed.
d: Management and IT skills are being considered as well as technical and legal issues.
e: Appropriate training records are maintained.

Practices should bear in mind the need for compulsory CPD in relation to the Law Society and other professional regulatory bodies. A firm committed to quality will see more to training than mere CPD compliance, but it is always a consideration nonetheless. There are also a number of requirements for designated supervisors and caseworkers in the SQM and LSC contracts that practices will need to consider if they hold a contract for publicly funded work.

Examples of major non-compliances

- There is no discernible training process within the practice.
- The process adopted by the practice is clearly and materially ineffective, for example, because it has not been implemented in relation to a significant number of partners or staff.

Example of minor non-compliances

- There are training processes within the practice that are substantially effective but some element required by this section has not been adequately addressed.

6 SUPERVISION AND OPERATIONAL RISK MANAGEMENT

Recent changes in the indemnity insurance market for solicitors have led to much greater interest in the areas of supervision and risk management in private practice. Many firms will be concerned to reduce the incidence or risk of claims and complaints against the practice, thereby improving the profile of the firm in relation to insurance renewals.

For the purposes of this section, operational risk management is the control and reduction of prosecutions, claims and client complaints against the practice. Areas such as health and safety or occupiers' risks are not covered here: they are the domain of section 4 on facilities and information technology.

Effective supervision will be a concern wherever there is a commitment to delivering a quality service. The role of partners or senior managers is often seen as being increasingly one of supervision rather than simply fee-earning. For many firms the contribution by junior fee-earners will be key to profitability. This, in turn, requires more emphasis on supervision than has generally been the case in the past.

Assessors should be aware of Practice Rule 13, which is not directly part of the Lexcel standard, but which is important for a general understanding of the framework within which solicitors are required to operate. This provides that every office where the solicitor practises from needs to be 'properly supervised'. This now includes a requirement that anyone assuming the responsibility for supervising that office should be trained to do so as set out in the Rule unless they were already in place as the office supervisor as at 23 December 1999, in which case phasing-in arrangements still apply.

6.1   Practices will have a written description of their management structure which designates the responsibilities of individuals and their accountability. This will be updated within three months of any change.

The description of management structure may take many forms, from the simple list of responsibilities commonly found in the introductory sections to the office manual to an organisational chart showing the role of departments and administrators in the overall reporting structure. In-house departments are required to show how the legal department fits into the parent organisation and the main reporting structures within the department. The management structure in a sole practice may be very simple as there may be only one person who is responsible for everything. All the functions for which the sole practitioner is responsible need to be listed.

Example of major non-compliances

- There is no description of the management structure or it does not reflect the reality within the practice.

Example of minor non-compliances

- There is a written description of the management structure but it is defective or inadequate to a limited extent, e.g. various key roles are not identified.

6.2   There will be a named supervisor for each area of work undertaken by the practice. A supervisor may be responsible for more than one area of work. The supervisor must have appropriate experience of the work supervised and be competent to guide and assist others.

Practices are required to designate a named supervisor for each area of work that they undertake. In many cases it will not be apparent from the full list of services provided; it will be a matter of judgement in every case as to whether a limited supply of work is a distinct aspect of work in its own right or merely an incidental part of a larger area of the practice's work. One example would be that change of name deeds would usually be seen as being incidental to certain areas of practice and not a distinct area of specialisation.

There are two separate limbs to the competences that supervisors must show: technical experience and supervisory skills. In relation to the first of these there are no particular requirements in the Lexcel standard, for example, for supervisors to be members of a specialist panel if one exists for that area of work, or to maintain a minimum number of hours of work per annum on that specialisation. Likewise, there is no requirement that supervisors must be of a certain status such as partner or senior manager.

By contrast, assessors will seek evidence of appropriate experience and training. The standard of experience will vary between those who 'self-supervise' and those who are responsible for large departments within a practice, especially if staffed by more junior personnel. Where a sole practitioner does not have solicitor or other experienced lawyer colleagues, or there is only one solicitor practising in a particular area of law within a larger practice, he or she is self-supervising. In such circumstances, the solicitor will need to demonstrate how supervisory skills are applied to his or her own professional development (for example, in planning the work programme and analysis of training needs).

Supervisors might wish to consider preparing a brief profile of their experience and recent training in the event that the assessor wishes to explore this with them.

Examples of major non-compliances

- There is no supervisor for all or some of the areas of the practice's work.
- One or more of the supervisors does not have the necessary experience of the work supervised to be able to guide and assist others.
- There is objective evidence that one or more of the supervisors does not have sufficient skills or experience of supervision to be able to guide and assist others, e.g. interview evidence with personnel in that department or a pattern of non-compliances on files inspected which were not known about.

Example of minor non-compliances

- One or more areas of work within the practice do not have designated supervisors but there are personnel who do perform the function and their role is merely not noted.

6.3   Practices will have processes to ensure that supervision of all staff, both legal and support staff, is effective. Issues which should receive consideration may include:

  a: Checks on incoming and outgoing post, including e-mails and faxes.
  b: Departmental, team and office meetings and communication structures.
  c: Reviews of matter print-outs in order to ensure good financial controls and the appropriate allocation of workloads.
  d: The exercise of devolved powers in publicly funded work.

Assessors will seek evidence from interviews that any arrangements for supervision are adequate. Particular attention will be paid to the availability of supervisors in multi-office practices. In most cases there must be more to availability than the supervisor simply being contactable by phone, though this might be adequate where it is senior personnel only who are supervised.

The proper allocation of work is a significant tool for quality control. This may be evidenced by a partner's signature to a matter opening form in private practice. Many practices will benefit from reviewing how introductions are referred internally where normal controls can sometimes be bypassed. In high volume areas of the practice, fee-earners will often be authorised to accept or decline instructions. However, the nature and number of open files will often be subject to discussion at supervision meetings.

Examples of major non-compliances

- One or more supervisors could not be seen to have been sufficiently available to attend to the needs for supervision that exist.
- There is no observable process for the appropriate allocation of work in one or more areas of the practice.

Example of minor non-compliances

- There are adequate processes for the availability of the supervisor and for the allocation of work but there has been a limited number of instances where they have not been observed.

6.4   Practices will have processes to ensure the effective supervision of legal work, to include:

  a: The availability of adequate supervision.
  b: Appropriate procedures to allocate new work and reallocate existing work if necessary.

Section 6.4 should probably be seen as the acid test of supervision: is it effective in the way that it operates within the practice? Assessors will compile evidence of the effectiveness of supervision from interviews with those who are supervised and from files inspected.

Common supervisory tools include those in requirement 6.3, as well as 'one-to-one' review meetings at regular intervals.

With the exception of file reviews (see 6.6) it is not mandatory that any particular supervisory tool is in place. The onus is on the practice to show that it operates appropriate supervision in each area of the practice, given the seniority and experience of those working in that area, the complexity of the work undertaken and the past record of mistakes, claims and complaints. There will often be quite different arrangements for separate areas within the same firm.

Assessors will make enquiries as to the effectiveness of supervision particularly in multi-office practices.

Supervision of support staff should ensure that people have suitable equipment and back-up facilities (see also 4.1); workloads are monitored; systems of work are appropriate; staffing, training and development, health and welfare needs of staff are met; and that staff have the opportunity to receive feedback and raise any issues of concern to them.

Example of major non-compliances

- There are clear inadequacies in the arrangements for supervision in one or more areas of work within the practice.

Example of minor non-compliances

- Although largely adequate, there is a limited number of instances where supervision has been inadequate or ineffective.

6.5   Practices will have processes to ensure that all those doing legal work check their files regularly for inactivity to avoid client dissatisfaction and possible claims arising from delay.

It is important that files are checked regularly by those handling them to ensure that client dissatisfaction and possible claims arising from delay do not occur. This requirement is ancillary to independent file reviews since those are normally carried out by someone who has not had conduct of the matter. In addition, file reviews tend to be selective and will not therefore check whether all matters are being progressed in an appropriate manner. Typical arrangements will include a weekly to monthly trawl by the fee-earner of the contents of their filing cabinet and/or e-mail records or a check of an accounts department print-out of all matters per fee-earner, especially if it is a report that highlights time elapsed since time recorded on that matter.

Examples of major non-compliances

- There are no processes for checking for inactivity in one or more areas of the practice.
- There are processes for checking for inactivity but they are widely ignored by a significant number of persons within one or more of the practice areas and there is evidence of delay in progressing matters.

Examples of minor non-compliances

- There are processes for checking for inactivity but they are being ignored by a limited number of personnel in one or more areas of the practice.
- The documented processes are being generally complied with but are not effective in preventing delay arising from inactivity in a limited number of instances.

6.6   Practices will have procedures for regular, independent file reviews, of either the management of the file or its substantive legal content, or both. The number and frequency of such reviews will be documented. There is no requirement that designated supervisors should conduct all such reviews in person, but they will need to show that they control or monitor the process and that the process is effective.

In relation to file reviews, practices will have procedures to ensure that:

a: A record of the file review is kept on the matter file and centrally, whether for the practice or office as a whole or by team or department.
b: Any corrective action which is identified in a file review must be actioned within 28 days and verified by the reviewer.
c: There is a review at least annually of the data generated by file reviews which will contribute to the review of risk assessment data (section 6.7f).

The main requirement in section 6.6 is for regular independent file reviews. These reviews need not be undertaken by the designated supervisor in person although they often will be; where the supervisor does not undertake all reviews in person it will need to be apparent that they will occur under the supervisor's control. The supervisor may delegate some of the checking to a non-fee-earner where he or she has appropriate experience and training.

File review arrangements will need to extend to all personnel, including partners and senior managers. The frequency and depth of reviews may reflect the seniority and experience of the file handlers. In most practices more file reviews are required for those with limited experience – perhaps up to three years' post-admission experience in the case of solicitors.

Ideally, file reviews are undertaken by someone other than the person with conduct of the case. However, in sole practices and where there is only one fee-earner practising in a category of law, it may not be possible to identify anyone who could comment on legal issues. Where such is the case, a supervisor, fee-earner in another category, suitably trained manager or administrator may carry out the file review. If a sole practitioner is the only fee-earner, the process of case management and client care activity can be reviewed by a member of support staff. Another option is that file reviews could be outsourced, as where there are reciprocal arrangements with fellow local sole practitioners. It will be important to ensure that client confidentiality is controlled in such cases, however, and that no conflict of interest arises from the operation of such arrangements.

The review will generally embrace technical and procedural issues but may be limited to procedural review only. This will be most common in sole or very small practices where there is no prospect of another person within the practice having the necessary expertise to assess the technical content of the file.

It is common practice to employ pro forma sheets for file reviews: for an example see the *Office Procedures Manual*. They will also highlight corrective action that is needed and record when it has been closed out. Corrective action will usually be checked by the reviewer on the files actually reviewed, or fee-earners may confirm that it has been carried out, but in some cases the corrective action might be checked at a future file review. One example could be the systematic failure of a fee-earner to send out satisfactory Practice Rule 15 initial information: it may be more expedient to check that this problem has been addressed by looking at a batch of files opened after the corrective action has been requested.

File review data should be assessed and will need to be seen as risk assessment data for the annual risk review required by the following section.

Example of major non-compliances

- There are no adequate file review arrangements in one or more departments of the practice.

Example of minor non-compliances

- There are file review arrangements in the practice but there is some inadequacy in their operation in one or more areas of the practice, for example:
    - There are limited instances of file reviews not being conducted as required in the case of some fee-earners.
    - The file review records are missing or incomplete with some fee-earners.

6.7 **For the purposes of this section, operational risk management is the control and reduction of prosecutions, claims and client complaints against the practice. Practices will ensure that procedures are in place to:**

    a: **Designate one overall risk manager for the practice with sufficient seniority, to be able to identify and deal with all risk issues which may arise.**

    b: **Establish appropriate reporting arrangements to ensure that risk issues are appreciated and addressed.**

    c: **Maintain lists of work that the practice will and will not undertake including any steps to be taken when work is declined on grounds that it falls outside acceptable risk levels. This information should be communicated to all staff and should be updated regularly.**

d: **Maintain details of the generic risks and causes of claims associated with the area(s) of work that is/are undertaken by the practice. This information must be adequately communicated to all staff.**

e: **Manage instructions which may be undertaken even though they have a higher risk profile than the norm for the practice including unusual supervisory and reporting requirements or contingency planning.**

f: **Conduct at least an annual review of all risk assessment data generated within the practice, including claims records, an analysis of client complaints trends and data generated by file reviews. The practice should identify remedial action which should then be reviewed at management level in the practice.**

This section addresses the need for clear management of operational risk in legal practice. It is based on the recommendations of the Turnbull report on the management of risk prepared by the Institute of Chartered Accountants for the Stock Exchange and now widely adopted in the business world at large.

The main requirement is that one designated person should have overall control of the risk exposure of the practice. This is not to say that that person needs to have all of the responsibility: in many firms different personnel will have the roles of handling complaints, claims and money laundering reporting, for example. In such instances the overall risk manager might be the managing or senior partner in private practice, or one of those with a particular responsibility. The overall risk manager should have sufficient seniority and influence within the practice to be able to ensure that risk matters are treated with the importance that they will usually deserve. In many firms these critical responsibilities are combined under the auspices of a compliance partner, sometimes the senior partner.

Assessors should appreciate that section 6.7 is likely to be of greater importance to private practice firms than to in-house practices. In many governmental or local authority practices the parent body will not have insurance in place and will, in effect, self-insure. Assessors should note that in-house practices may not be able to decline instructions (see also guidance in relation to 8.2). However, there may still be risks which may need to be managed, for example adopting an effective media strategy in potentially sensitive matters. Therefore, in the interests of providing a reliable and satisfactory service to clients, the requirements of this section must still be addressed.

There are a number of authoritative works on risk management. Copies of the Solicitors' Indemnity Fund Self Assessment Questionnaire can be purchased from the Law Society bookshop.

One familiar suggestion in risk management is that the organisation should be more selective in the work that it takes on. There should be evidence that consideration is always given to whether the practice has sufficient resources and expertise to meet the client's reasonable expectations. Work that is beyond the competence of the practice, where mistakes are more likely to happen, should be declined and, if possible, referred elsewhere.

Practices will need to compile and keep under review lists of the risks implicit in the work that they undertake. This should be based primarily on the experience of the practice.

Where work is accepted into the practice even though it has a higher risk profile than the norm there should be special procedures to ensure that particular care is taken with it. One example is a matter that might seem to be quite straightforward, but where the potential loss in the event of a negligence claim would be at the upper end of the firm's maximum liability cover and might even exceed it. These risks should be known about from the start and be carefully managed throughout.

It is important that the practice learns from its experience and continues to look to improve its profile where possible. There needs to be an annual documented review, therefore, of all risk assessment data. This will include:

- Complaints data.
- Information on claims and notifications to the practice's insurers.
- File review data.
- Client survey findings and any other information which might be helpful.

The format of this report is for each practice to determine for itself. It may be presented as an item at a regular strategic meeting or be independent from it. Steps should be taken to share the findings with all personnel within the practice.

Example of major non-compliances

- There are no processes in effective operation to manage risk associated with work accepted, declined or undertaken by the practice.

Examples of major non-compliances in relation to this section are more likely where there is a general failure of various of the requirements listed within the section or a number of failures within one or more of the departments.

Examples of minor non-compliances

- There is no overall risk manager in place but such an individual could readily be appointed.
- There are processes in effective operation which cover the requirements of this section but they are not documented or the documentation is defective.
- The practice has not listed the areas of work that it will undertake and decline in one or more of its practice areas.
- There are no lists of generic risks associated with an area or areas of the practice's work or they have not been reviewed in the last 12 months.
- There are no arrangements to manage work of an unusually high risk profile in one or more of the areas of work of the practice.
- No annual review of risk assessment data has been compiled in the last 12 months but it should be possible to compile this from the data available within 21 days.

6.8   Operational risk needs to be considered in all matters before, during and after the processing of instructions. Before the matter is undertaken the adviser must:

    a: Consider if a new client and/or matter should be accepted by the practice, in accordance with section 8.2 below.

    b: Assess the risk profile of all new instructions and notify the risk manager in accordance with procedures under 6.7 of any unusual or high risk considerations in order that appropriate action may be taken.

During the retainer the fee-earner must:

c: **Consider any change to the risk profile of the matter from the client's point of view and report and advise on such circumstances without delay, informing the risk manager if appropriate.**

d: **Inform the client in all cases where an adverse costs order is made against the practice in relation to the matter in question.**

At the end of the matter the fee-earner must:

e: **Undertake a concluding risk assessment by considering if the client's objectives have been achieved and if the client could fairly complain or make a claim for damages in relation to the service provided.**

f: **Notify the risk manager of all such circumstances in accordance with documented procedures without delay.**

The essence of section 6.8 is that risk needs to be considered before, during and after the work is performed for the client.

An initial risk assessment should be based on the instructions received. Special risk will then need to be referred to the risk manager via a procedure established for doing so. This could either be a risk notice or a section in the matter opening form highlighting 'high' or 'unusual' risk associated with the instructions or the client.

During the retainer the ongoing risk profile should be considered. If the risk to the client or the firm changes materially – e.g. third parties are joined onto litigation, materially adding to costs risks, or counsel's opinion is obtained casting doubt on advice already provided to the client – the client will need to be informed and consulted without delay. Adverse costs orders need to be reported immediately as they will usually have to be paid forthwith.

At the end of the matter the fee-earner should consider if the client could fairly claim or complain about the service provided. This is not as simple as looking at whether the transaction or litigation succeeded or not, but rather whether the client could feel that they were not as effectively represented as they might reasonably have expected. In such circumstances there will need to be a procedure for a report to be made to the risk manager. All such reports could be addressed initially to a departmental supervisor, such as the head of department.

Examples of major non-compliances

- Risk is routinely overlooked before, during or after the matter is undertaken in one or more of the areas of work undertaken by the practice, such that risk management procedures are not in effective operation.
- Reports of risk are made but are not being acted upon or assessed by the risk manager or someone to whom he or she delegates responsibility to do so.

Examples of minor non-compliances

- There are limited instances in one or more areas of the practice of risk not being considered before, during or after the matter is undertaken.
- Reports of risk have in some instances been overlooked or not acted upon.

7 CLIENT CARE

The importance of client care has received extensive coverage in recent years. For the individual practice the significance is readily apparent: in a competitive profession the quality of service to the client will bear heavily on whether to instruct that firm again on future occasions. For the profession more widely, the threat remains that if standards of client service are judged inadequate, the reputation of the profession may be adversely affected.

Assessors will not simply seek evidence of client care procedures being in place, but will also want to see evidence that there is a culture within the practice that recognises the importance of client care and seeks to improve service standards wherever possible. Practices should be truly client-centred: a token approach to client care systems will not be adequate. To make this a reality, top management will need to recognise its role in giving a clear lead on the standards of service delivery that will be expected.

Key issues

- The current approach to client service and where improvements could be made.
- Adoption of a client care policy.
- Extent of involvement of staff and/or clients in the development of a client care policy.
- Compliance with Practice Rule 15 and the Solicitors' Costs Information and Client Care Code.
- How precedent letters on costs information and client care issues could be improved.
- Whether current complaints procedure meets the guidelines established by the Office for the Supervision of Solicitors.
- Who should take responsibility for client surveys and when and how they should be carried out.

7.1   Practices will have a documented policy for client care, which will include:

> **a: The practice's commitment to provide services to clients in an appropriate manner.**
> **b: Procedures to ensure compliance with Practice Rule 15 and its accompanying code in relation to client care and costs information.**

The requirement for a client care policy is in line with recommendations from the Office for the Supervision of Solicitors. Its recommendations on the development and adoption of a client care policy can be found in 'Keeping clients', a client care guide for solicitors. This can be viewed on the Law Society website **www.clientcare.lawsociety.org.uk**. It will be for each practice to determine its approach to the style and format of documentation and, in particular, whether it forms part of a more general policy document or is produced separately. Given the extensive overlaps between related management concerns the client care policy might be styled as the 'risk management' or the 'quality' policy in many firms.

The sort of issues that should be addressed, whatever the description of the documentation, will include:

- Responsibility for client care.
- General approach of the firm.
- Actions that will be taken to test and improve client care.
- Specific procedures as required by the other provisions of this section.

Examples of major non-compliances

- The policy on client care is so defective that it is not in effective operation or it seriously fails to address a number of the relevant issues of client care in that practice.
- Interviews within the practice, perhaps in conjunction with other data, suggest that there is insufficient commitment to the policy by most personnel in the practice. It would be possible to record a major non-compliance against a department where there was evidence of a lack of commitment to client care by a majority of personnel within it.

Examples of minor non-compliances

- There are processes in effective operation which cover the requirements of this section but they are not documented or the documentation is defective.
- There is a documented policy on client care but it does not cover or deal adequately with some element that is relevant to the practice.
- Interviews within the practice, perhaps in conjunction with other data, suggest that there is insufficient commitment to the policy in some quarters.

7.2 **Practices will have processes to ensure that clients are informed in writing of the terms of business under which instructions are received and will be handled, including:**

    a: **The name and status of the fee-earner and the person(s) responsible for overall supervision.**
    b: **Whom the client should approach in the event of a problem with the service provided.**
    c: **The basis under which charges will be calculated including the best information possible on the likely overall costs of the matter.**

    The information required by this section should usually be provided in writing unless there are professional considerations that make this unsuitable in any particular matter.

    There must be a record of any standing terms of business with regular clients, such as many commercial clients. The practice must be able to produce such terms in relation to the issues covered by this section.

Practices are reminded of the risks of not informing clients of the status of the fee-earner handling their matter: see *Pilbrow* v. *Peerless de Rougemont* [1999] 3 All ER 355 where the Court of Appeal ruled that the provision of advice by a non-solicitor, where advice from a solicitor had been specifically requested, meant that no fees were recoverable by the firm for the work done for the client.

The obligation in the Lexcel standard in relation to initial information on complaints by clients is limited to the need to ensure that clients are aware of whom they should approach in the event of a problem with the service provided. This does not necessitate the full complaints procedure to be set out in initial correspondence. In many cases it would be inappropriate to do this, especially if the client is in some distress at the time of instructing the practice.

This requirement reflects the relevant provisions of the Solicitors' Costs Information and Client Care Code which, in turn, sets out how practices will comply with Practice Rule 15 where appropriate.

Assessors will take into account that 'employed solicitors' (i.e. in-house practices) are not obliged to follow rules 3–6 of the Code, which deal with the provision of initial and continuing costs information to clients, but should 'have regard' to these provisions (2e of the Code). A local authority that provides advice and services to other separate authorities may well be in much the same position as a private practice and would need to address these requirements.

In cases of apparent conflict between the Lexcel standard and the provisions of the Code the latter should take precedence. In particular, assessors are reminded of the provisions of 2b of the Code which provides that strict compliance with its requirements will not be required in every case, such as:

- repetitive work for a repeat client where the client has already been provided with the relevant information, although such clients will need to be informed of changes (e.g. changes to charge out rates that will apply to this work in future); or
- in all cases where compliance with the Code would be 'at the time insensitive or impractical'.

Commercial departments may well establish standing terms of business with their key, regular clients. The practice must be able to produce such terms in relation to the issues covered by this section. Situations where assessors may not expect the Code to be complied with immediately could include probate instructions where a recent death has occurred or complex instructions where some initial investigatory work will be needed in order to provide the client with helpful and reliable information. In such circumstances the Code envisages that 'relevant information should be given as soon as reasonably practicable' (2b:ii).

In most situations the provision of hourly rates without reference to the likely total time that may be incurred on the matter will not amount to the 'best information possible on the likely overall costs of the matter'. Hourly rates would not usually be quoted to clients where these do not form the basis on which fees will be calculated, such as in fixed fee work or domestic conveyancing work that will be charged on an estimate basis. Practices are referred to the provisions of rule 4c–e of the Code on what might amount to 'best information possible' and to:

4f–g: The basis of the firm's charges.
4h–i: Further information required.
4j: The client's ability to pay and the source of funding.

4k: Cost benefit and risk.
5: Additional costs information for private paying and publicly funded clients, including potential liability for third party costs.

Example of major non-compliances

- The practice fails in a significant number of instances to confirm any or all of the issues dealt with by this section where it would be appropriate to do so or it fails to do so in any practice area (e.g. one department consistently fails to do so).

Examples of minor non-compliances

- There are a limited number of instances where all or some of the issues dealt with by this section are not confirmed to clients where it would be appropriate to do so.
- There are arrangements to agree standing terms of business with regular clients but these are not sufficiently accessible to people within the firm needing to consult them.

It is envisaged that where a very limited number of files only do not comply with these requirements this would be noted as an area for improvement in the report.

7.3   Practices will operate a written complaints handling procedure that:

a: Is made readily available and accessible to clients when it is apparent that they may wish to have recourse to it.

b: Defines what the practice regards as a complaint and sets out how to identify and respond to complaints.

c: Records and reports centrally all complaints received from clients.

d: Identifies the cause of any problem of which the client has complained, offering any appropriate redress, and correcting any unsatisfactory procedures.

Practices must conduct reviews at least annually of complaints data and trends, such review(s) forming part of the review of risk assessment under 6.7f above.

It is a requirement of the Solicitors' Costs Information and Client Care Code 1999 that:

'Every principal in private practice must … have a written complaints procedure and ensure that complaints are handled in accordance with it; and ensure that the client is given a copy of the complaints procedure on request.' (7b)

A precedent complaints procedure can be obtained from the Practice Standards Unit by contacting tel: 01527 883264. The leaflet is called 'Handling complaints effectively'.

Practices will need to determine how they will define what a 'complaint' is. A wide definition of 'any expression of client dissatisfaction, however it is expressed' will result in more numerous instances of having to report to the practice's system. An unduly restrictive definition – e.g. that it has to be in writing – may not be regarded as adequate by the Office for the Supervision of Solicitors. Assessors should be satisfied that the approach adopted by the practice is appropriate for its client base.

Reports to the central system could be pro forma or by e-mail or another format. The complaints handler need not be the risk manager of the practice but often the roles will be undertaken by the same person. Where there are separate roles of complaints handler and risk manager it is a requirement that the reporting of one to the other should be clearly documented (see 6.7b).

It may be more difficult for sole practitioners to provide clients with an opportunity to express dissatisfaction to someone who is not actually involved with the matter if there is no other lawyer or senior member of staff. Where there is another senior member of staff he or she may respond to any complaint in relation to the principal. In some areas, and where there is no risk of conflicts of interest, sole practitioners act as complaints officers for each other's firms. In addition, some local Law Societies operate an independent informal mediation service between their members and clients.

The annual review of complaints data may form part of a review of the business plan. Whatever approach is adopted for the review it will be necessary for the practice to show that the report has received proper attention from senior management.

Examples of major non-compliances

- The complaints handling process is seriously deficient in some major regard so that it cannot be said to be in effective operation.
- The records of complaints are so badly or inadequately maintained that the complaints handling system cannot be said to be in effective operation.
- There is widespread ignorance of the practice's approach and procedures on complaints handling amongst people within the practice.

Examples of minor non-compliances

- There is a complaints handling process which is in effective operation but it is not documented or the written complaints handling procedure is deficient in some way, e.g. it fails to define what the practice regards as a 'complaint'.
- There has been no annual review of complaints data outside the 12 months stipulated.

7.4   Practices must conduct an annual review to check that the practice's commitment to provide quality services is being met in the perception of clients.

Some form of client survey to test satisfaction with the services provided must have occurred within the 12 months preceding the assessment or annual maintenance visit. This need not be continuous nor need it involve all parts of the practice. There must, however, be adequate data on which the practice can assess the effectiveness of the delivery of its services.

The practice should specify how and when clients will be requested to provide feedback and the methodology it will use to analyse it. The findings and outcome should be documented. Any client feedback data could be added to the review of risk assessment data under 6.7 and the review of the quality system under 1.6.

Example of major non-compliances

- There has been no client survey conducted over the 12 months preceding the assessment or the annual maintenance visit. In any such instances some form of survey will need to be collected, and considered by senior management, before the non-compliance can be closed out.
- The information collected in the 12 months preceding the client survey or the annual maintenance visit, having regard also to evidence collected in previous years, is not adequate for the firm to assess how well it is delivering its services.

Examples of minor non-compliances

- The client survey data has not received appropriate attention from top management.

8 FILE AND CASE MANAGEMENT

The final section of the Lexcel standard may prove to be the most time-consuming to implement. The practice will need to review how its legal files are organised and set down clear standards that must be adhered to. Those fee-earners who are most set in their ways may struggle to comply with any new requirements, but the improvement of file standards may well be the single greatest benefit to come from a Lexcel programme. This section is best viewed as tracking the life of a file from start to finish: from first enquiry to eventual archiving.

Key issues

- Handling of client enquiries.
- Acceptance of new clients and new matters from existing clients.
- Arrangements for conflicts of interest.
- How instructions are taken, recorded on file and confirmed.
- Planning the progress of a matter.
- Ensuring that matters are progressed in an appropriate manner.
- The giving, monitoring and discharge on undertakings.
- Traceability of files, papers, deeds and other documents – also items that come into the firm's possession or control.
- How counsel and other experts are chosen, instructed, evaluated and paid.
- File closing and archiving.

8.1   Practices will document how client enquiries in relation to possible instructions are handled, with particular regard to:

a: The treatment of telephone enquiries.
b: Clients who enquire in person in the reception area, including confidentiality.
c: Enquiries by correspondence and e-mail.

There will be very different considerations for practices in relation to initial enquiries. A firm that attracts work from callers off the street will probably need more elaborate arrangements than the in-house department where work is transferred by e-mails from colleague departments.

Many firms let themselves down at the first enquiry stage by having no clear arrangements for handling enquiries about possible instructions. It is all the more important to plan how enquiries will be handled in areas such as domestic conveyancing where telephone quotations are an important source of work for most firms.

Similar considerations apply to clients who enquire in person in the reception areas. When seeking information about the potential client's enquiry, it is nevertheless important to ensure that confidentiality is respected (see also 8.9c). Sadly, all practices open to public access should consider staff safety and how threatening or abusive behaviour should be dealt with.

In relation to enquiries by correspondence or e-mail, practices might establish a minimum response time, in which case this will be taken into account by assessors. There might also be a general enquiries file that all such messages are stored in. Many conveyancing departments keep notes of all enquiries in order to monitor success rates from quotations provided.

Example of major non-compliances

- There are documented arrangements for handling initial enquiries but they are not in effective operation or the arrangements do not reflect actual practice within the firm to a significant extent.

Examples of minor non-compliances

- There are arrangements for handing initial enquiries which are in effective operation but they are not documented.
- There are documented arrangements for handling initial enquiries but they do not reflect actual practice within the firm to a limited extent.
- The documented arrangements are defective in some regard, e.g. there are no documented arrangements for telephone enquiries or clients who call in person or enquiries by correspondence or e-mail.

8.2 Practices will document how decisions will be made whether to accept new instructions from existing clients or instructions from clients who have not instructed the practice before.

In most firms greater attention will be paid to the acceptance of new clients than new instructions from existing clients. Where there is any policy of declining work, for example in relation to the financial viability of the work or past experience with that client, this must be documented. Practices may not decline to act for reasons that would amount to a breach of policies of the Law Society in relation to anti-discrimination or equal opportunities.

Assessors should be aware that there is no 'cab-rank' principle in relation to work accepted by solicitors in private practice.

Assessors will accept that in-house practices may not be able to decline instructions. Where acceptance of instructions may cause difficulty (see also requirement 6.7), they should have systems to draw such issues to the attention of senior decision-makers within the umbrella body. However, where in-house practices act for legally separate entities, they must comply with the Employed Solicitors Code and procedures for dealing with such clients should reflect those of private practices.

The reasons why a practice might decline work should be set out in the office manual and could include:

- Work is not of a specialisation that the firm undertakes.
- Work would not be sufficiently profitable or meet firm's strategy.
- Work could be of a type that the firm does not wish to be associated with (e.g. pornography).

- Conflict of interest, professional or commercial.
- Past record of unsatisfactory experience with this client.
- An individual or department is operating at capacity.

Practices will need to consider who can decide if and when work should be declined, whether from existing or new clients, and document if and how this will be relayed to the potential or existing client. It should be noted that *The Guide to the Professional Conduct of Solicitors 1999* provides that a firm should not accept work where a solicitor has insufficient time, experience or skills to deal with instructions. The 1999 edition of the *Guide* provides at page 245 under the chapter on 'Retainer' that 'a solicitor must not act, or continue to act, where the client cannot be represented with competence and diligence'.

Example of major non-compliances

- There are documented arrangements for evaluating whether to accept instructions from new or existing clients but the arrangements are not in effective operation or they do not reflect actual practice within the firm to a significant extent.

Examples of minor non-compliances

- There are documented arrangements for evaluating whether to accept instructions from new or existing clients but they are defective in some way, e.g. it is the practice's policy to accept instructions in respect of intellectual property matters but this is not documented.
- There are documented arrangements for evaluating whether to accept instructions from new or existing clients but these have not been followed to a limited extent, e.g. it is the practice's policy that accepting a certain type of matter must be authorised by a partner and this has not been followed in one particular case.

8.3   Practices will document their arrangements to ensure that conflicts of interest are identified and acted upon in an appropriate manner. Although this is a particular consideration when receiving instructions it may also be an issue later in the matter, as when third parties are subsequently joined in proceedings.

A conflict of interest would prohibit a practice from acting for a given client. Where two established clients wish to deal with or claim against each other it is likely that the firm will not be able to act for either. The limited circumstances where a conveyancing department could act for seller and purchaser are provided for in Practice Rule 6 and its accompanying guidance in *The Guide to the Professional Conduct of Solicitors 1999*.

In some departments conflicts of interest will not arise or will be very unlikely, e.g. the practice offers a service in immigration law and would never act for the Home Office. It follows that very different procedures might be in place for different departments within the same firm. Conflicts of interest are remote in in-house legal practices since the department will, in effect, represent one client only.

Although conflict most obviously arises as an issue at the outset of a matter it could develop at any stage and fee-earners need to be alert to the dangers of conflicts developing once work has started on the matter.

Practices may choose to extend arrangements on conflicts of interest to include commercial considerations. This is most likely with larger commercial practices where a particular client may seek an exclusivity agreement (that the firm will not represent other businesses in that sector).

Examples of major non-compliances

- The documented procedures are used so inconsistently that they are not in effective operation in one or more departments within the practice.
- There is little or no evidence that conflict of interest procedures have been followed and therefore the practice cannot demonstrate that they are in effective operation.

Examples of minor non-compliances

- Procedures for considering conflicts of evidence are in effective operation but they are not documented.
- There is a limited number of instances of fee-earners who are not giving due consideration to conflicts of interest.
- There is a limited number of instances of fee-earners who are not following the documented procedures for conflict checking.

8.4   At the outset of the matter the fee-earner will establish:

   a: As full an understanding as possible of the client's requirements and objectives (where incomplete this must be supplemented subsequently).
   b: A clear explanation of the issues raised and the advice given.
   c: What the fee-earner will do and in what timescale.
   d: Whether the fee-earner is the appropriate person to deal with the matter or whether it should be referred to a colleague.
   e: Method of funding, including the availability or suitability of insurance, trade union benefits, conditional or contingency fee arrangements or costs insurance products.
   f: Whether the intended action would be merited on a cost benefit analysis and whether, in public funding cases, the guidance in the funding code would be satisfied.

   The issues covered in a–f above must be confirmed to the client, ordinarily in writing, unless it would be appropriate not to do so under the Solicitors' Costs Information and Client Care Code. In all cases a note of these issues must appear on the matter file.

The importance of a clear start to the matter file should be readily apparent. Likewise, a clear note at the start of the matter file setting out all pertinent details and the instructions received should always be a priority. The fee-earner must note not only the instructions but also the client's objectives. All too often there is no clear note of the first meeting or conversation. Confusion, errors and embarrassment can result from this.

If a contemporaneous letter or e-mail to the client confirms all issues that would have been covered in the first meeting or communication it could be accepted as an adequate note of the meeting. The date and time of any meeting must be referred to, however, and this is best achieved through an attendance note. The availability of computer time records might also be taken into account.

It will not always be possible to confirm all details with confidence at the outset (e.g. timescale) in which case the advice might be outline and confirmed as soon as it becomes clearer.

In relation to 8.4d, a document confirming the name and status of the person who has conduct of the matter (see 7.2a) is acceptable evidence that the issue of suitability has been considered.

Some practices may operate general files in relation to some instructions. For example, in-house practices may have general files in which they record enquiries from instructing departments. Where such is the case, assessors will expect to see criteria which set out when a matter specific file should be opened. Similarly, in private practice, telephone only duty solicitor attendances in crime are usually filed together by date rather than by opening an individual matter file.

In private practice, rule 4j of the Costs Information and Client Care Code provides that, 'the solicitor should discuss with the client how when and by whom any costs are to be met'. This rule goes on to place an obligation on the fee-earner to consider the various methods of funding that could be available to the client, including those mentioned in 8.4e. It is important that solicitors cover these matters and note them on file in order to minimise the risks of a 'lost opportunity claim' in which the client later asks why the possibility of relying on existing legal expenses insurance or other source of funding was not raised earlier. It is good practice to confirm the client's instructions on the availability of insurance, trade union benefits, etc. in a letter to the client.

In publicly funded (legal aid certificate) matters the funding code provides a two-stage test. First, the practitioner must assess the prospects of success, ranging from 'very good' (above 80%) to 'unclear' (where representation will be refused). If prospects are borderline, a Representation Certificate will be refused unless there is a significant wider public interest (i.e. the case will benefit a group of individuals wider than the client) or the case is of overwhelming interest to the client (i.e. it is about life, liberty, or the roof over his/her head).

If the case can be quantified, the cost benefit must then be determined in relation to the prospects of success. For example, if prospects are very good, likely damages must exceed likely costs, whereas if prospects are moderate, likely damages must exceed likely costs by a ratio of 4:1. In unquantifiable cases, such as claims other than for damages, having regard to all the circumstances, the likely benefits must justify the likely costs such that a reasonable private paying client would be prepared to bring or defend the case. In 'public interest' cases, having regard to all the circumstances, including the prospects of success, the likely benefits to the client and others must justify the likely costs.

In all matters in private practice it is important that the fee-earner considers whether the likely outcome will justify the likely expenditure by the client (see rule 4k of the Costs Information and Client Care Code). Although this rule does not apply to in-house lawyers consideration should always be given even by the non-private practice adviser as to whether a court might make a costs order to reflect its disapproval of the use of the court's time on the matter in question.

In-house practices may comply with the requirements of this section by way of a document which is distributed to client departments. Such a document may also cover other procedures, e.g. charges (see 7.2c and 8.5), complaints (see 7.2b), document and deed storage arrangements (see 8.9b and 8.11d). Any exceptions to this overall agreement must be confirmed in writing to the client department.

Examples of major non-compliances

- The documented procedures required by 8.4a–f are used so inconsistently that they are not in effective operation in one or more departments within the practice.
- There is little or no evidence that the procedures have been followed and therefore the practice cannot demonstrate that they are in effective operation.

Examples of minor non-compliances

- There are procedures for all the requirements of this section which are in effective operation but they are not documented.
- There are documented procedures for all the requirements of the section but one or more elements of them is/are not being followed in a limited number of instances or by a limited number of fee-earners.

8.5 Practices will ensure compliance with the requirements of the Solicitors' Costs Information and Client Care Code in relation to initial costs information and, in particular, the provision of the 'best information possible on the likely overall costs of the matter, including a breakdown between fees, VAT and disbursements' (4a). Where there are special circumstances making the provision of this information inappropriate the special considerations must be noted on the matter file. In relation to standing agreed terms with regular clients see section 7.2.

This section should be read in conjunction with section 7.2. It stresses the need for full costs information at the outset of a matter save where exempt under section 2 of the Code, such as where repetitive work is done for a repeat client who has already been provided with the required information.

In some cases it may not be possible to give an estimate of total costs at the outset, for example in a medical negligence matter where an expert's report may be required to establish that the client has a cause of action. In such cases, an estimate of the cost of initial steps should be provided.

Where time forms the basis on which costs will be calculated, practices may provide information about hourly rates and the likely number of hours to be taken or may provide an estimate as a range of costs, e.g. between £500 and £1,000. In such matters, giving clients a list of hourly rates without providing a calculation of likely costs is unlikely to be acceptable.

Examples of major non-compliances

- There are no arrangements for the confirmation of initial costs information in one or more departments of the practice.
- The documented procedures are used so inconsistently that they are not in effective operation in one or more departments within the practice.

Examples of minor non-compliances

- There are arrangements for the confirmation of initial costs information which are in effective operation but they are not documented or the documentation is defective.
- There are arrangements for the confirmation of initial costs information but there are a limited number of files or fee-earners who are not complying with all or some of the requirements.

8.6   Practices will ensure that the strategy for the matter is always apparent on the matter file and that in complex cases a separate case plan is developed. Save in exceptional cases the client must be consulted upon and kept informed of the strategy in the matter and any planned changes to it.

All matters must have a clear strategy. In most cases this will be apparent and will need only a letter to the client confirming what the practice proposes to do. In other, more complex, matters a separate case plan is required. In publicly funded (legal aid) matters, any case requiring an individual high cost case contract (whether civil or criminal) must have a separate case plan.

Examples of situations where assessors would not expect clients to have been consulted on changes to the case plan or strategy could include cases where the firm acts for a minor or in certain mental health cases. However, where a litigation friend or guardian has been appointed to act on someone's behalf, an assessor will expect him or her to be consulted and informed.

It is important the client is kept abreast of proposals on the strategy for the matter and, save in exceptional matters (for example, those involving minors where someone is acting on their behalf), is in agreement with it.

Examples of major non-compliances

- There are no observable processes setting out the strategy for matters in one or more departments of the practice.
- There are numerous instances of there being no strategy on matters.
- There are numerous instances of the client not being informed or consulted on the strategy where they could reasonably expect to be so involved.

Examples of minor non-compliances

- There is a limited number of files where no strategy is apparent.
- There is a limited number of files where the client has not been consulted on and/or informed of the strategy and/or changes to it.

8.7   Practices will have documented procedures to ensure that matters are progressed in an appropriate manner. In particular:

    a: Key information must be recorded on the file.
    b: Key dates must be recorded on the file and in a back-up system.
    c: A timely response is made to telephone calls and correspondence from the client and others.
    d: Information on cost is provided at least every six months and, in publicly funded matters, the effect of the statutory charge, if any, is provided to the client in accordance with the Solicitors' Costs Information and Client Care Code.
    e: Clients are informed in writing if the person with conduct of their matter changes, or there is a change of person to whom any problem with service should be addressed.

Section 8.7 requires practices to ensure that matters are progressed effectively. All too often matters 'drift' when the initial work has been done. Delay remains one of the principal causes of complaint to the OSS.

Whether 'key information' is shown on the file will depend on any particular arrangements in place for the practice. It has become increasingly common to have a file summary sheet, which could be combined with a progress check in various areas of work, but this would probably be too basic for very substantial files running to numerous lever arch files. On the other hand, a very straightforward matter with few documents, attendance notes or correspondence, may not need a schedule or file summary sheet. The standard for this section is that the file (with any accompanying data records which form part of the practice's filing system) should tell the story of what is going on in that matter. Very often this will be achieved through systematic noting of all actions and conversations in relation to that matter by way of attendance notes.

Key dates should be seen as any date, which, if missed, could give rise to a claim against or a loss by the practice. There are key dates in all areas of legal work: it is for every practice to determine its list of relevant key dates. All key dates must be noted on the file (which could include data records where these form part of the filing arrangements in question). They will often be highlighted in any file summary sheet, but do not necessarily need to be so. However, where they are not, they must still be readily apparent to anyone reading the file or accessing the data record.

The back-up system for key dates is increasingly likely to be a computer-based system, but the fee-earner's personal diary may be accepted if it does not leave the practice's premises. Where a hard copy diary is used for this purpose a departmental or team diary would generally be seen as being preferable.

In assessing whether sufficient information has been given on the progress of matters and a timely response has been made to telephone calls or correspondence the assessor will take into account any instructions or preferences that the client has expressed in this regard (8.7c–e). Where a firm stipulates response times (e.g. all telephone calls from clients to be returned within 24 hours) they will be assessed on this basis.

The requirement to provide a costs update every six months reflects rule 6a of the Costs Information and Client Care Code. It should be remembered that there is no need to provide a routine costs update every six months if the client has agreed otherwise. This agreement could be implied in work that has an annual cycle, e.g. annual trusts and investment work. Section 8.7 gives effect to sections 6c–d in the Costs Information and Client Care Code.

Checking for inactivity could take various forms including a weekly or monthly trawl through the filing cabinet or a print-out review by the fee-earner or his/her supervisor, especially if this highlights time lapsed since time was last recorded to that matter.

If a solicitor practises as the only fee-earner, it is not necessary to have a documented procedure to inform clients about any change in the person with conduct of the matter.

Examples of major non-compliances

- There are no processes covering the majority of requirements of the section in relation to progressing matters.
- The documented procedures are used so inconsistently that they are not in effective operation in one or more departments within the practice.

Examples of minor non-compliances

- There are processes covering the requirements of the section in relation to progressing matters which are in effective operation but they are not documented or the documentation is defective in some respect.
- There are documented procedures for all the requirements of the section but one or more elements of them are not being followed in a limited number of instances or by a limited number of fee-earners.

8.8   Practices will document procedures for the giving, monitoring and discharge of undertakings.

An undertaking is defined in *The Guide to the Professional Conduct of Solicitors 1999* as 'any unequivocal declaration of intention addressed to someone who reasonably places reliance on it and is made by: (a) a solicitor or a member of a solicitor's staff in the course of practice; or (b) a solicitor as "solicitor", but not in the course of practice'. Failure to honour an undertaking is described in the *Guide* as being, prima facie, professional misconduct which could be dealt with at a disciplinary tribunal and enforceable by the courts through their inherent jurisdiction.

It should be noted that:

- An undertaking need not be described as such.
- In private practice an undertaking will be binding on the partners even if they did not know of or sanction it.

- In certain circumstances liability could arise from an undertaking given in the solicitor's private life.

Given the potential liability that could be suffered, practices will wish to consider when and how undertakings should be provided. Common arrangements will be to distinguish routine and non-routine undertakings and apply different safeguards to them. Conveyancing departments are likely to specify who can provide routine undertakings on exchange and completion of contracts. Consideration should be given to the procedure for authorising undertakings required by a court as practicalities may require special arrangements.

There is no requirement for a central register of undertakings though some practices find this helpful. Many practices check that any undertaking has been discharged as part of their file closure procedures (see also 8.11).

Examples of major non-compliances

- There are no processes for the giving, monitoring and discharge of undertakings.
- The documented procedures are applied so inconsistently that they are not in effective operation in one or more departments within the practice.

Examples of minor non-compliances

- There are processes in effective operation which cover the requirements of this section but they are not documented or the documentation is defective.
- There are documented procedures for all the requirements of the section but one or more elements of them are not being followed in a limited number of instances or by a limited number of fee-earners.

8.9   Practices will have a documented procedure to:

> **a: List open and closed matters, identify all matters for a single client and linked files where relevant and all files for particular funders.**
> **b: Ensure that they are able to identify and trace any documents, files, deeds, wills or any other items relating to a matter.**
> **c: Safeguard the confidentiality of matter files and all other client information.**
> **d: Ensure that the status of the matter and the action taken can be easily checked by other members of the practice.**
> **e: Ensure that documents are stored on the matter file(s) in an orderly way.**

Most practices will be able to identify the funders of matters (e.g. the Legal Services Commission, named trade unions or legal expense insurers) through a computer coding system.

Conveyancing departments should be able to link sale and purchase files for the same client in linked transactions.

As a general rule all papers relating to a matter should be capable of being traced by being on the file. When a file is contained in a number of folders/lever arch files, there should be some method by which they can be shown to belong to the same matter. This could be by use of the client/matter reference number and an indication on each part, e.g. 1 of 2; 2 of 2, etc. or 'correspondence from 01.01.03 – 09.09.03' or by listing on a schedule, kept in a prominent part of the file. Where there are ancillary papers or other records (e.g. X-rays or medical records in clinical negligence work) they should be linked to the file in question by tagging or use of the client/matter numbering system.

Consideration should be given to all the circumstances where safeguarding the confidentiality of the client could be at risk (e.g. files being worked on during a train journey, files left in unattended cars, etc.). Where clients are seen in the reception area there should be arrangements for consultations, even if very short, to be conducted out of earshot of other clients or visitors in the reception area.

The state of matter files is important under this section. Showing key information on a file summary sheet or colour coding of notes of meetings, reviews or letters to the client are helpful options. Where computer case management systems are used, the assessor will need to check the procedures for naming and storing documents and for taking regular back-ups.

Assessors will judge the tidiness of files under 8.9e. In order to comply with this requirement, attendance notes need to be filed in date order and papers need to be secured within the file. Attendance notes in cardboard folders should be secured on 'treasury tags' or other fastenings. More substantial documents may be placed together in file pockets, plastic wallets or similar.

Examples of major non-compliances

- There are no processes for one or more of the requirements of the section in relation to file status.
- The documented procedures are used so inconsistently that they are not in effective operation in one or more departments within the practice.

Examples of minor non-compliances

- There are processes in effective operation which cover the requirements of this section but they are not documented or the documentation is defective.
- There are documented procedures for all the requirements of the section but one or more elements of them are not being followed in a limited number of instances or by a limited number of fee-earners.

8.10 Practices will have a documented procedure for using barristers, expert witnesses and other external advisers who are involved in the delivery of legal services, which will include provision for the following:

   a: Use of clear selection criteria, which do not discriminate on grounds of race, colour, ethnic or national origins, sex, creed, disability, sexual orientation or age.
   b: Where appropriate, consultation with the client in relation to selection, and proper advice to the client on choice of advocate or other professional.

c: **Clients to be advised of the name and status of the person being instructed, how long she/he might take to respond, and where disbursements are to be paid by the client, the cost involved.**

d: **Maintenance of records (centrally, by department or office) on barristers and experts used, including evidence of assessment against the criteria.**

e: **Evaluation of performance, for the information of other members of the practice.**

f: **Giving of instructions which clearly describe what is required and which, in litigation matters, comply with the rules of court and any court orders.**

g: **Checking of opinions and reports received to ensure they adequately provide the information sought (and, in litigation matters, comply with the rules of court and any court orders).**

h: **Payment of fees.**

Where outsiders to the practice are involved in the service provided, checks should be in place to ensure that the practice's commitment to quality is still assured.

It is necessary for the practice to maintain lists of counsel and other experts used. This may be one list for the practice as a whole or it could be devolved to the departments or teams within the practice to maintain their own lists.

Lists are never closed: it should always be possible to add newcomers. The list will be a useful first point of contact; where counsel or an expert are used for the first time, checks should be made as to their suitability, and a note made on file of why they have been instructed. When appropriate, consideration should be given as to whether to include that provider on the approved list.

Many practices might be interested to maintain a non-approved list. The combination of the rights of the data subject and the law of defamation mean that this should be very carefully controlled. However, such a list can avoid counsel or an expert being instructed subsequently, when he or she has already failed to meet the practice's quality standards.

There will need to be procedures for how instructions are provided and checked. The client's consent to the instruction of an outsider would usually be needed, not least so that they can express any preference and understand the implications for the fees that they will or may have to pay.

Procedures for paying fees are likely to differ depending on the way cases are funded.

Examples of major non-compliances

- There are no processes for the requirements of the section in relation to the use of counsel and experts.
- The documented procedures are used so inconsistently that they are not in effective operation in one or more departments within the practice.

Examples of minor non-compliances

- There are processes in effective operation which cover the requirements of this section but they are not documented or the documentation is defective.

- There are documented procedures for all the requirements of the section but one or more elements of them are not being followed in a limited number of instances or by a limited number of fee-earners.

8.11   Practices will have documented procedures to ensure that, at the end of the matter, the practice:

  a: Reports to the client on the outcome and explains any further action that the client is required to take in the matter and what (if anything) the practice will do.
  b: Accounts to the client for any outstanding money.
  c: Returns to the client any original documents or other property belonging to the client if required (save for items which are by agreement to be stored by the practice).
  d: If appropriate, advises the client about arrangements for storage and retrieval of papers and other items retained (in so far as this has not already been dealt with, for example in terms of business) and any charges to be made in this regard.
  e: Advises the client whether they should review the matter in future and, if so, when and why.
  f: Archives or destroys files in an appropriate manner.

It is essential that matters are closed effectively. In most firms a reminder and checklist is provided for the issues covered in this section either on the file summary sheet (see the *Office Procedures Manual*) or in an archiving instruction sheet.

Those with conduct of cases should also remember to conduct a final risk assessment to consider if there are circumstances that should be reported to the practice's risk manager. If a sole principal is the person responsible for risk management, a note of any such circumstances should still be made in relation to his or her own files as this information contributes to the annual review of risk (see also 6.7f). In private practice noting issues of concern at the end of a matter might necessitate a report to the firm's insurers.

The Law Society does not advise on any particular period for the retention of files before they are destroyed but practices should note that the Money Laundering Regulations 2003 require certain records to be kept for at least 5 years. The Legal Services Commission stipulates as a term of its criminal and civil contracts that files must be retained for six years after closure.

Examples of major non-compliances

- There are no processes for the requirements of the section in relation to file closure and archiving.
- The documented procedures are used so inconsistently that they are not in effective operation in one or more departments within the practice.

Examples of minor non-compliances

- There are processes in effective operation which cover the requirements of this section but they are not documented or the documentation is defective.

- There are documented procedures for all the requirements of the section but one or more elements of them are not being followed in a limited number of instances or by a limited number of fee-earners.

Appendix

Summary of substantive changes in Lexcel 2004 version

2004 Lexcel		2000 Lexcel
Structures and Policies	1	–
Constitutional framework	1.1	–
Business framework considered and reviewed	1.2	–
Risk management strategy or framework	1.3	–
Written quality policy	1.4	–
Management responsibility for quality	1.5	–
Review of operation of quality system	1.6	–
Non-discrimination policy	1.7	B.2
Equal opportunities and diversity	1.8	D.8
Money laundering compliance	1.9	–
Mortgage fraud prevention	1.10	–
Data protection compliance	1.11	–
Health and safety policy	1.12	E.1
Strategy, the Provision of Services and Marketing	2	
Marketing and business plan(s)	2.1	B.1a, B.1c
Service plan	2.2	B.1b
Review of plans above	2.3	B.1d

2004 Lexcel		2000 Lexcel	
Financial Management	3		
Responsibility for financial procedures	3.1	C.1	
Financial processes	3.2	C.2	Need for documented procedures removed: processes now acceptable
Annual budget	a		
Variance analysis of budgets	b		
Profit and loss accounts	c		
Balance sheet	d		
Cashflow/funds forecast	e		
Variance analysis of cash/ funds flow	f		
Time recording	3.3	C.3	Need for documented procedures removed: processes now acceptable
Facilities and IT	4	E	
Use of premises and equipment	4.1a		
Photocopying	b		
Clients visiting offices	c		
Staff facilities	d		
Mail, fax and communication	e		
Finance procedures	f		
Document review of health and safety	4.2	E.1b, E.1c	
Business continuity plan	4.3		
Information technology plan	4.4		Formed an element of B.1a
Purchasing, etc.	a		
Current and planned applications	b		
Data protection compliance	c		
Compliance	d		
User safety	e		
E-mail use and storage	f		
Computer data and system back-up	g		Formed an element of E.1a

2004 Lexcel		2000 Lexcel	
Legal research and library; updating of information	4.5	E.3	
Office manual	4.6	E.2	
People Management	5		
Recruitment and development plan	5.1		Recruitment and development plan was an optional element under D.1.1
Recruitment needs	a		
Training and development	b		Training and development planning was a requirement of D.5
Welfare and entitlements	c		
Job documentation	5.2	D.1	Now extends to partners also
Recruitment	5.3	D.2	Required documented arrangements or recruitment areas to be covered now more specific
Verification of vacancies	a		
Drafting of job documentation	b		
Methods of attracting candidates	c		
Selection methods	d		
Storage of interview notes	e		
Information to unsuccessful candidates	f		
Other information sources	g		
Confirmation of job offer	h		
Maintenance of communication pre-joining	i		
Induction process	5.4	D.3	Required documented arrangements process now acceptable. Contents of induction made more specific
Practice aims	a		
Management structure and individual's responsibilities	b		
Terms and conditions; personal details	c		
Initial and future training	d		

2004 Lexcel		2000 Lexcel	
Key policies	e		
Induction process to be held in reasonable time of taking role	5.5		
Induction on changing roles internally	5.6		
Process for annual review of responsibilities, objectives and performance	5.7a	D.4a, D.4b	Now applies to partners also and does not need to be a documented procedure
Process for appraisal records	b	D.4c	
Process for training review	c	D.5b	
Provision of appropriate training	5.8	D.5	
Supervision and Operational Risk Management	6		
Written description of management structure; update within 3 months	6.1	A.1	
Named supervisor for each area of work	6.2	A.1	
Process for effective supervision	6.3	D.7	
Supervision of legal work	6.4	F.10	
Adequate supervision	a	F.10a	
Allocation of work	b	F.10, F.10b	
Checking for inactivity	6.5	–	
File reviews	6.6	F.10c	
Record of file review on file and centrally	a	F.10d	
Corrective action	b	F.10	28 day rule now introduced
Review of file review data	c	–	
Operational risk management	6.7		

2004 Lexcel		2000 Lexcel
One overall risk manager	a	F.1f (i)
Reporting arrangements	b	F.1f
Lists of work not undertaken	c	F.1f (v)
Generic lists	d	F.1f (ii)
Unusual risk matters	e	F.1f (iv)
Risk assessment data reviews	f	F.1f (vi)
Operational risk	6.8	
Client acceptance	a	–
Risk profile of new instructions	b	F.4f
Change to risk profile	c	F.5c
Addressee costs orders	d	F.5f
Concluding risk assessment	e	F.7f
Notify risk manager	f	F.7g
Client Care	7	
Client care policy	7.1	–
Commitment to provide services	a	
PR15 compliance	b	F.3
Terms of business	7.2	F.3
Role and status of fee-earner and supervisor	a	F.4a (v)
Problem with service	b	F.4c
Basis of charges and best information possible	c	F.3
Written complaints handling procedure	7.3	F.11
Available to clients	a	F.11b
'Complaint' defined	b	F.11a
Report and review complaints	c	F.11c
Response to complaints	d	F.11d
Annual review	7.4	–

2004 Lexcel		2000 Lexcel	
Case and File Management	8		
Handling of client enquiries	8.1	E.1	Implicit in E.1
Telephone enquiries	a	–	
Client enquiries at reception	b	–	
Written enquiries	c	–	
Decisions on new clients	8.2	–	
Conflicts of interest	8.3	F.16	
Outset of matter	8.4		
Client requirements and objectives	a	F.4a (i)	
Explanation and advice	b	F.4a (ii)	
What fee-earner will do	c	F.4a (iii)	
If matter to be transferred to colleague	d	–	
Method of funding	e	F.3 (iii)–(x)	
Cost benefit analysis	f	F.4e	
Initial costs information	8.5	F.3	In particular F.3 (i)
Strategy and case plan	8.6	F.4a (iv)	
Progressing matters	8.7		
Key information on file	a	F.9c	
Key dates on file and on back-up system	b	F.1d, F.4d	
Timely response	c	F.5d	
Costs updates	d	F.5e	
Change of person handling matter	e	–	
Undertakings	8.8	F.1e	
Matter management	8.9		
List open and closed files	a	F.1a, F.2	
Traceability	b	F.6	
Confidentiality	c	–	
Status apparent	d	F.9a	
Orderly filing	e	F.9b	
Use of barristers and other outside advisers	8.10	F.8	

2004 Lexcel		2000 Lexcel
Selection criteria	a	F.8a
Consultation with client	b	F.8c (b)
Name and status of adviser instructed	c	–
Records on advisers	d	F.8c
Evaluation of performance	e	–
Clear instructions	f	F.8d
Checking of opinions	g	F.8e
Payment of fees	h	F.8f
End of matter	8.11	F.7
Report on outcome	a	F.7a
Account for monies	b	F.7b
Return of documents	c	F.7c
Storage and retrieval	d	F.7d
Future review	e	F.7e
Archive and destruction	f	

Index